Gren. Jackson.

THE GEOGRAPHY OF BUSINESS CYCLES

A Case Study of Economic Fluctuations in East Anglia, 1951-68

Morgan Sant

London School of Economics and Political Science

ISBN 0 85328 018 5

Printed by Goron Pro-print, Churchill Industrial Estate, Lancing, Sussex.

Foreword

One of the aims of this series of monographs is to give a wider circulation to pieces of research which might otherwise remain unpublished. Dr. Morgan Sant's work deserves to be more widely known. He has made a novel exploration of the impact of business cycles on the distribution of rates of unemployment in East Anglia. Earlier workers have collected much evidence about regional cycles, but Dr. Sant believes the scale of analysis should be shifted to subregional variations. He has attempted to examine variations at this scale in the amplitude and timing of responses.

The basic data for the study are the unpublished monthly returns of male unemployment for the exchange areas of East Anglia from 1951 to 1968. The appeal of the work is perhaps mainly to academic research workers concerned with processes of regional change and development. Some of the findings may be specific to East Anglia but additional analysis of other regions should produce generalisations valid at a national level. Dr. Sant has not set out to produce results of direct value to regional planners but his work has relevance to their problems. Cyclical responses are found to be strongly related to geographical factors.

Dr. Sant experienced difficulties resulting from data limitations and may have felt disappointed at times along the way. The final result is its own tribute to his persistence and to his scrupulous standards in method and argument.

J. E. Martin

Preface

This monograph is based on research largely conducted during three fruitful years as a post-graduate in the Geography Department at the London School of Economics. During that time I was fortunate to have many stimulating contemporaries as well as a supervisor, Dr. J. E. Martin, whose criticism and encouragement have proved of lasting value.

My thanks are also due to the government departments for providing information and to the Central Research Fund of London University for financial support to carry out surveys.

MORGAN SANT,
Norwich 1972

Contents

List of Figures

I

Introduction

This study begins from two beliefs; first, that a geographical approach to business cycles is a valuable adjunct to understanding their form and composition; second, through the analysis of cycles it is possible to gain greater insight into the processes of regional change and development. In the wider context this study can be related to three recent developments. The first is a resurgence of interest in the geography of business cycles which, in contrast with earlier work, has been concerned with spatial rather than regional models. Two important examples are Haggett's study of south west England[1], and the work of King, Casetti and Jeffrey in the American Mid-West.[2] Next, increasing interest in regional forecasting has created a demand for studies of the dynamics of regional change. In particular, there is a critical need, well described by Harvey,[3] to escape from static equilibrium models and to take full account of leads, lags and asymmetrical responses to given conditions of development. Finally, growing attention has been given to the spatial distribution of welfare, thus giving a valuable underpinning to more mechanistic studies of production and distribution. If this study contributes towards a wider knowledge in each of these fields it will have achieved its purpose.

This study is concerned with subregional variations in the response to cyclical fluctuations, and is based upon the hypothesis that such variations are a function of the spatial structure and industrial composition of a region. Unfortunately, at this scale it is not possible to trace the source and transmission of cycles (probably the key issue in the whole field of business cycles), and attention is largely confined to variations in the amplitude and timing of responses.

The region chosen for the study is approximately the administrative counties of Norfolk, Suffolk and Essex, which together cover about 5000 square miles, and had a population of about 2·0 million. Although, in comparison with other regions, East Anglia has a relatively simple economic landscape, there are a number of important dichotomies which might be expected to be reflected in cyclical movements. Thus, distinctions can be drawn between urban and rural areas, manufacturing and service-dominated towns, rapidly-expanding and declining areas, zones which are close to London and those which are remote, and so on. The sub-regional divisions used in the study were determined by the form of the basic data, the unpublished monthly returns of male unemployment, which were available for the forty-five exchange areas covering the region, in an unbroken series from March 1951.

Finally, it has occasionally been questioned whether business cycles, *sensu strictu,* still occur in the post-Keynesian world. Indeed, the problem was put directly in a recent collection of papers edited by Bronfenbrenner;[4] the consensus was strongly affirmative. Since 1945 the British economy has experienced four complete cycles during which unemployment has tended to conform with movements in other series, varying nationally from about 4 per cent during recessions to below 1·5 per cent during booms. These may not seem very large figures, but they represent the difference between quite rapid growth and near stagnation in the national economy.

References

1. Haggett, P. (1971) Leads and lags in interregional systems: a study of the cyclic fluctuations in the South West economy; in *Spatial Policy Problems in the British Economy,* edited by M. Chisholm & G. Manners, London.
2. King, L. J., E. Casetti & D. Jeffrey (1969) Economic impulses in a regional system of cities: a study of spatial interaction. *Regional Studies,* 3, 213-8.
3. Harvey, D. (1971) Social processes, spatial form and the redistribution of real income in an urban system, in *Regional Forecasting*, edited by M. Chisholm, A. Frey & P. Haggett, London.
4. Bronfenbrenner, M. editor (1969) *Is the Business Cycle Obsolete?* New York.

II

Cycles in Space

The study of business cycles has a long history which can be roughly divided into a number of phases. Through the nineteenth century the chief concern lay in noting the occurrence of cycles, measuring their periodicity and exploring their relationships with other phenomena. The early decades of the twentieth century saw major, but often conflicting efforts to develop aggregative endogenous models. More recently there has been a shift in emphasis towards disaggregative studies, with a strong empirical bias.

Seen in historical perspective, the content of these studies has generally been closely related to the problems of the time and place at which the work was being conducted. As a result, in the 170 years since Herschell[1] postulated a causal chain from solar variations ("sunspots"), through harvests and food prices to demand for non-agricultural goods, at least five different periodicities and causes have been claimed. These include innovation waves (50 year periodicity),[2] construction and population (20 years),[3] agricultural (10 to 15 years),[4] investment (7 to 11 years)[5] and inventories ($3\frac{1}{2}$ years).[6] Each of these contains much of interest and at least two, agricultural and construction/migration cycles, have strong geographical connotations. Thus Jevons postulated "the singular connection between the prosperity of Lancashire and the price of rice in India",[7] and Habbakuk concluded that "English urbanization alternated with American colonization;"[8] both statements applied to nineteenth century conditions. However, since 1945 cycles in Britain have tended to recur at short intervals, associated with domestic production and investment and the trade balance.[9]

Regional Cycles

National cycles can be regarded as the product of changes in many different sectors; for example, Mitchell[10] analysed nearly 800 series for the United States and Mitchell and Deane[11] have collected several hundred British series covering periods up to 150 years. Alternatively, the national cycle can be disaggregated into regional components, with the rate of change in national series interpreted as a parameter of the frequency distribution of changes in the array of regions.[12] Moreover, regional analysis, like sectoral analysis, can take account of the various cyclical components (timing, conformity . . . etc.), as a means of identifying the degree of regularity of behaviour in regional systems.

In the study of regional cycles two major sets of questions arise: first, why do regions have cyclical fluctuations? Second, what regional variations can be identified, and what causes them? Frequently, the first of these is overlooked, or its answer implicitly assumed, but it is apparent that a variety of forces can affect business conditions and, hence, the nature of regional cycles. Thus, in theory at least, answers to the first question will contribute to the solution of the second.

A classification of forces affecting business conditions proposed by Neff[13] consists of the following categories.

(*a*) Nationally uniform forces, such as changes in taxation and monetary policy or the availability of technical innovations.

(*b*) Nation-wide forces with discriminatory regional impacts.

(*c*) Forces originating in specific regions, with an effect transmitted to other regions, e.g. the discovery or exhaustion of a resource.

(*d*) Forces which are localised and contained within a specific region.

While it is clear that all four can cause regions to have cycles there is, unfortunately, no indication of their relative importance, either conceptually or empirically. Kidner[14] queried the significance of the two last sets of forces, suggesting that they are generally minor and that, for regions, the sources of cycles tend to be exogenous and imprecise in their geographical origins; this is especially so if regions are small. Nevertheless, this is a useful classification for it distinguishes forces which lead to synchronized behaviour from those which cause divergence. The balance between these sets determines the geographical extent of a cycle, but the operation of any one of them alone is enough to cause a fluctuation in a region.

The concept of transmission of cycles, emphasised in Neff's third category but associated also with the first two, has its foundations in international and interregional trade theory, and is associated with Keynesian income analysis.[15] Simply, regions derive a part of their incomes from sales to other regions plus monetary remittances, 'foreign' investment, and so on. Changes in these sales (i.e. exports) lead subsequently, via the multiplier, to changes in investment and consumption, part of which is in the form of reduced imports from other regions. The whole system is a multi-regional circular flow with, in theory, equilibrium levels for all its parameters, so that for any region the effect of transmitted changes in income can be derived from an equation incorporating the interregional trade multiplier:

$$\triangle Y = \triangle (I - M_i + E_i + E_c) \frac{1}{1 - c'(1 - q')} \quad \ldots\text{Equation 1}$$

(after Vining)[16]

where Y is change in income and the terms on the right of the equation are investment (I), imports of capital goods (M_i), exports of capital and consumer goods and services (E_i) and E_c), and the multiplier, $1/1 - c'$ $(1 - q')$. The denominator of the final term is the marginal propensity to import goods and services. Assuming the parameters for each region to be different these relationships explain regional variations in the transmission of changes.

Transmission of fluctuations has two aspects – timing and amplitude. In the case of timing, the factor determining when the turning points in a series occur (say, in response to a nationally uniform force) is the behaviour of exports. When a change in income occurs consumers are selective in their responses; demand for some goods and services changes immediately while for others the change is more gradual or may not occur at all. The result is also regionally selective, for producers of many of the goods and services are concentrated in a few regions comprising their "basic" or export sectors.[17] Thus if a region produces goods for which the marginal propensity of other regions to import is high, and if other regions have a high income elasticity of demand, the impact will be more rapidly experienced than in a region with the opposite conditions.

Ideally it would be possible to identify and explain a chain of events in which one region after another received and transmitted changes in demand during a cycle. Indeed, in several studies[18] the turning points in regional cycles have been investigated, but with little or no positive results. This lack of success is due to several factors. First, the problems faced in any attempt to reconstruct the transmission process accurately are insurmountable, and the next-best solution, analysis of leads and lags, has been inconclusive. Secondly, most cycles have been associated with nationally uniform causes which, in the twentieth century (though not necessarily in earlier cycles), have been diffused rapidly: it appears to be only in the mildest cycles that variations in timing are most obvious. Thirdly, the speed with which information is circulated through mass media makes it likely that responses anticipate real changes in demand, so that in cycles, especially in employment, regions tend to act together: that is, "expected transmission" substitutes for actual transmission.

The second aspect of the transmission process concerns the amplitude of fluctuations, and here evidence is much stronger and more consistent with theory. To explain why regional variations in income or employment occur during cycles, all past studies have been concerned, directly or indirectly, to explain the components on the right side of Equation 1. Again, economic base theory tends to be employed and in the majority of studies industrial structure is the first variable to be investigated, since it determines the magnitudes of E_i and E_c, and indirectly, M_i and M_c, if consumer patterns are assumed to be homogeneous. That is, an exporter of one commodity is, by implication, either self-sufficient in, or an importer of, others. In sum, the greater the basic sector in a region's economy, the more volatile other regions' propensities to import its products, and the less able the region is to pass on changes in demand (due to its own low propensity to import), the greater will be its vulnerability to cyclical fluctuations transmitted from other regions, and *vice versa*. Experimenting with values for these parameters, mining[19] produced striking variations in an hypothetical four-region model, in which two regions were given characteristics conducive to stability and two to instability.

It is a feature of economic base theory that regions with the same basic sectors, selling to the same markets, should have similar cyclical movements. Analysing ranked groups of states in the United States, Vining[20] found considerable regional similarities: the most volatile states were the producers of primary industrial products (cotton and coal), and investment and consumer durable goods. Borts,[21] using a "shift and share" analysis found that differences in amplitude were significantly correlated with industrial structure. Also of interest, he found that the differences between states' amplitudes tended to diminish between 1910 and 1950, due partly to the occurrence of milder cycles at the latter end of the period and partly to the industrial diversification of states.

However, it is clear that measures of industrial structure have never produced a complete explanation of regional variations, although it is evidently a more powerful factor than Neff considered on the basis of his analysis of only half-a-dozen industrial cities in the United States.[22] First, as Vining suggested, two regions with industrial similarity may present quite different time series, because "the markets in which are sold the products of their export industries may be, and perhaps for most commodities are, different for the two regions".[23] Secondly, there are other factors which affect regional economic behaviour, causing industrial structure to leave unexplained residuals. The most important of these would appear to have been, (*a*) regional variations in the strength of individual industries, (*b*) the underlying growth trends of regional economies, (*c*) the role of property incomes, (*d*) transport costs, and (*e*) occupational mobility. In addition, the role of inter-regional migration can also be listed.

Intra-industrial variations in unemployment have been postulated as major contributors to regional variations in cyclical sensitivity among British standard regions by Harris and Thirlwall, [24] though their explanations have been behavioural rather than locational, emphasis being placed on labour hoarding, and distribution and sensitivity of branch plants and labour mobility. Borts[25] also found significant intra-industry variations, and noted that they became larger, relative to inter-industry variations when cycles were most mild.

The significance of secular growth is more equivocal in theory, and the evidence is conflicting. Steiner[26] argued that secular growth and stability should be positively correlated in major cycles since growth implies industrial strength, although during minor recessions, when the main change is in inventories, he expected faster growing areas to react relatively more strongly. But in general evidence of significant relationships is weak, although it sometimes appears that the relationship might be quadratic rather than linear, (i.e. both fastest and slowest growth areas being volatile), and there is also a tendency for retardation in the rate of growth to be correlated with increasing vulnerability.

Inter-regional migration plays a part not only in the growth process leading to changes in demand for services and residential construction and increasing the supply of labour for basic and non-basic industries, but also adds to regional variations in fluctuations. An example, argued by Nordling,[27] concerns the origin of the 1929 Great Depression in the United States. Throughout the 1920's population increased and (more important) changed its distribution rapidly. In response, the construction industry expanded too much and in the wrong places, with the result that the eventual crash was all the more disastrous, and was a major factor in the general depression.

Cycles in the economic landscape

At the regional scale described above most studies have taken place within the framework of the Keynesian system and international trade theory. However, at the sub-regional level these are insufficient and it is valuable to begin by considering the role of spatial structure in the pattern of cyclical responses. For this purpose the Löschian "economic landscape"[28] is invoked, not because it is the only way of proceeding but because it provides a theoretical framework within which to develop hypotheses. What follows, therefore, is a discussion of variations in the amplitude and timing of responses, and possible directions of transmission. This is carried out in a stepwise manner, starting from the most simple landscape and dropping assumptions as shown in Table 2.1.

Table 2.1 Assumptions and stages in the development of a geographical theory of cycles.

Stages: (1) Simple economy
(2) Closed hierarchy
(3) Open, modified hierarchy
(4) "Real" economy

Assumption	Stage 1	State 2	State 3	Stage 4
single activity	1	0	0	0
isotropic surface	1	1	0	0
ubiquitous resources	1	1	0	0
perfect occupational mobility	1	1	1	0
identical consumer demand	1	1	1	0
homogeneous population	1	1	1	0
identical demand and supply elasticities	1	1	1	0
no substitution of materials/products	1	1	1	0
perfect competition	1	1	1	0

notation: 1 assumption made
0 assumption removed

Stage 1: A simple Economy

At its most simple level the landscape contains only a single activity—farming—which is distributed among an evenly-spaced population (which is assumed, initially, to be working at full capacity). What sort of economic cycle might be found under these conditions? Immediately it is possible, given the simplicity of the system, to discount all those which are fundamentally economic causes, whether endogenous or exogenous, since all units in the landscape are self-sufficient. All that can occur to upset the continuum is an exogenous shock, such as a variation in climatic conditions, which may or may not affect all units alike; but whichever is the case there will be no transmission of changes.

Such self-sufficiency, however, is rare, if it exists at all. Evidence of primitive economic systems, past and present, [29] indicates quite intricate trading patterns, and although the sector engaged in trade may not be large it is nonetheless open to changes transmitted from other regions. This first stage can therefore be regarded only as a hypothetical condition from which increasingly complex systems vary by growing degrees.

Stage 2: A Closed Hierarchical System

Abandoning the assumption that there is only one activity, the system which evolves as the Löschian economic landscape develops is that of a symmetrically distributed hierarchy of settlements and market areas which owes its form to the variations in the thresholds and ranges of different goods and services. Aggregatively the region has now a more diverse economy, but diversification varies between the ranks in the hierarchy. For simplicity it may be assumed that there are three ranks of place—city, town and village—and three activities—services, manufacturing and agriculture. Only the city contains all three functions; towns have the two latter; villages are entirely specialised in agriculture. Although Lösch was concerned mainly with the market areas of centrally produced goods and services, movements in the reverse direction can also be postulated with (say) food being produced in the lowest ranking centre for sale in the highest where local supply is less than demand.

Implicitly, such a system is dynamic. Hierarchies depend on the creation of new activities, and the new investment necessary to support them is likely to be directed disproportionately towards the higher ranking centres, where most new functions will be located. In addition to variations in the industrial structure of the three ranks there are also likely to be differences in their marginal propensities to consume local and imported goods and services. Identical consumer demand was assumed and from varying levels of specialization it will follow that the city will have the highest marginal propensity to consume local products and the villages will have the lowest. With identical elasticities also, it can be inferred that multiplier effects will be lowest in the former places and highest in the latter.

The breakdown of self-sufficiency leads to vulnerability to alternative causes of fluctuation. First an exogenous cause, as in the previous section, can again be postulated: second, an endogenous cause brought about by a falling marginal efficiency of capital can be invoked. The eventual outcome in both cases will be similar, but the paths through which it is reached will differ, especially at the onset of the cycle.

If it can be assumed that an exogenous change leads to an ubiquitous fall in production in the agricultural sector it follows that all three ranks will be affected but the impact will be relatively greatest in the villages. Successive phases in the cycle then show a number of transmitted effects. Villages, due to loss of income, reduce their demand for manufactured goods and services, affecting the towns and city, (the former to a greater extent). Subsequently, towns further reduce their demand for the services of the city, which in turn may reduce its imports from the lower ranks, and so on.

In this case the timing of the initial movement will be the same for all places, though the change may be barely perceptible in the city. The direction of transmitted changes will be predominantly centripetal, from the villages to the city. Finally, the amplitude of fluctuation is greatest in the villages and least in the city, correlating with the proportion of each rank's activity in the first-affected sector and, subsequently, with their propensity to consume local products.

The second alternative is a fall in investment. Here the initial impact is greatest in the city, but the effect will be rapidly diffused. However, transmission will be selective, not only by rank but also by distance from the initial location of reduced demand (Figure 2.1). The city, for example, not only produces some of its own food, but also imports a proportion from the villages. When demand falls the most vulnerable part of the agricultural sector will be that located furthest from the city, incurring the highest transport costs and receiving the lowest producer prices (Figure 2.2). That is, transmission is direct from the city to the most distant villages where, because of their specialization, the effect is likely to be great. Thereafter, the sequence of events is similar to that in the exogenously determined cycle.

In the second case variations in timing have been introduced, with the city leading. Amplitude, likewise, will be greatest at the beginning of the downswing in the city, but thereafter a deeper depression will probably occur in the villages—particularly the peripheral ones.

Stage 3: Open, Modified Hierarchy

It is next necessary to abandon two of the crucial Löschian assumptions, ubiquitous resources and the isotropic surface. When this is done the economic landscape contains opportunities for sub-regional specialization of a new kind. Whereas previously specialization was between ranks it can now develop between regions on the basis of localized resources. It is assumed that two sub-regions are served by a single regional capital in Region A and that trade occurs with Region B...

Given this system, and assuming an externally initiated fall in demand, what repercussions will be experienced in Region A?

This will depend, first, on the relationships between the specialized enclave and the remainder of Region A, and Region B. That is, how much of its trade (exports and imports) are conducted with the different areas, and the routes through which they pass. Several alternatives exist; trade may be concentrated with one partner, or shared between A and B, and if trade occurs with B it may pass directly to it, or be routed through the regional capital of A. In addition the enclave is likely to consume at least the high order services produced in that city. Within this framework the effect of a change may range from the enclave absorbing practically the whole of the impact, to its being only a fairly distinctive area in the overall response of Region A. To simplify, the effects can be investigated under three different sets of conditions:

(*a*) where the enclave trades only with Region B, using the city as an *entrepot*,

(*b*) where all the enclave's exports go to B, but where at least some imports come from the remainder of A,

(*c*) where there is a three-way trade between A, B, and the enclave.

In the first case the most significant change is experienced by the enclave. As a localized activity any downward shift must also be localized, especially as (with one exception) the enclave imports nothing from the rest of A. The exception is the use of *entrepot* services provided by the regional capital, which will also suffer an immediate

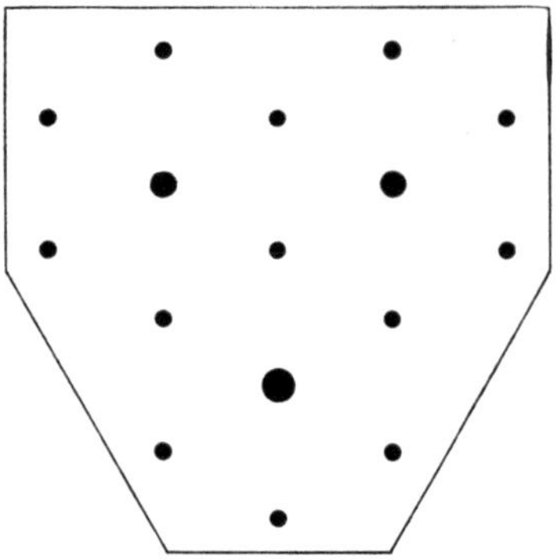

Fig. 2.1. Full employment in a closed, hierarchical economy.

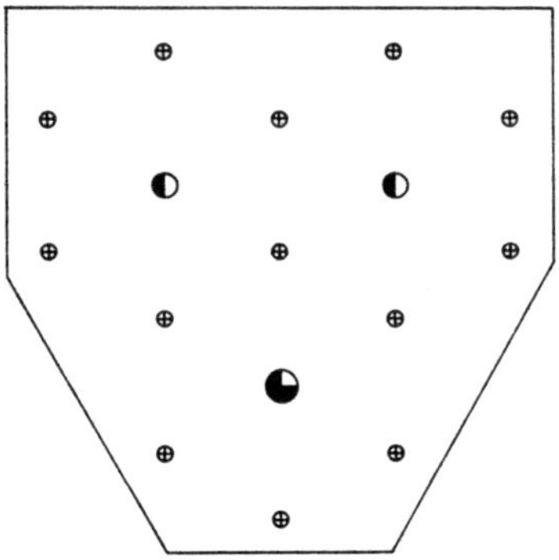

Fig. 2.2. Impact of a recession without transport costs.

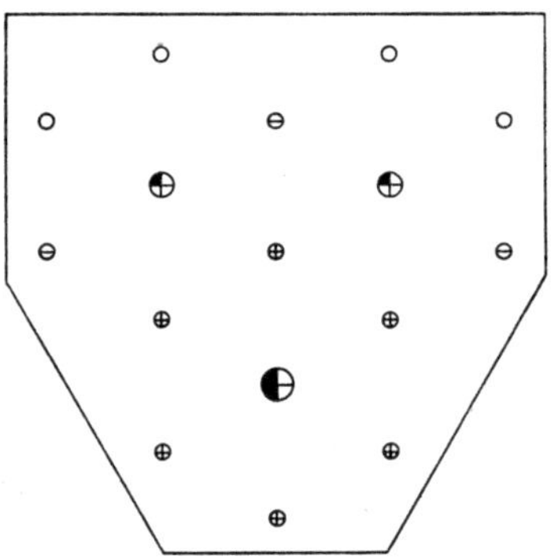

Fig. 2.3. Impact of a recession with transport costs.

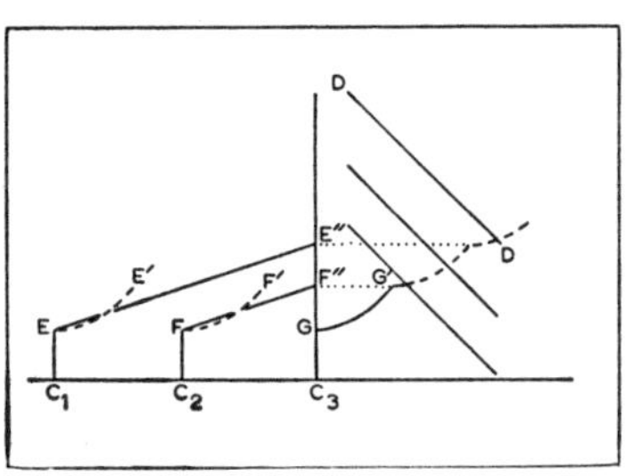

Fig. 2.4. The role of transport costs.

Notes (*a*) DD is demand.

(*b*) C_1 C_2 C_3 producers of commodity C.

(*c*) Market is located at C_3

(*d*) EE′, FF′ average

(*e*) EE″, FF″ transport costs to market.

down-turn, which may be transmitted to lower ranks in the hierarchy, but this is unlikely to be important.

The second case is an extension of the first, the only difference being a greater amount of trade between the enclave and the rest of Region A. Concomitantly, any contraction in B will be transmitted via the enclave more forcefully, and probably more speedily, especially if the enclave imports from A's low order centres in addition to the trade with the city.

In the third instance it is assumed that both sub-regions in A export to B, but that the initial reduction in demand is for the non-enclave's product's. The result is a reversal of timing, compared with the second case, with a contraction in the metropolis and the lowest order centres (the latter being responsible for exports of arable products). Thereafter, the effect is transmitted to other places, including the enclave, It is likely, but not inevitable, that the contraction will be most marked in the villages which, though not necessarily more specialised than the enclave, suffer from a decline in both markets (i.e. Regions A and B) at an early stage. The impact on the enclave depends mainly upon the marginal propensity of the remainder of Region A to import its products and the proportion of its output exported to A.

Stage 4: A "Real" Economy

In approaching the more realistic conditions for this stage it is necessary to abandon the remaining assumptions.

First, the removal of identical demand and supply elasticities produces two effects. Unequal demand elasticities give rise to further variations in the transmission of cycles. Faced with a given decline in their (equal) incomes individual and group substitution functions may differ between commodities. The effect is geographical where commodities are localised: the more localised the industry and the higher the elasticity, the greater will be the impact for a given fall in consumer incomes. Similarly, supply elasticities may vary; given a fall in price per unit of product industries may react in different ways. Those with lower elasticity will respond by reducing output (and employment) relatively less than those with high elasticity. Again, localization of industries, in association with their supply elasticities, will produce a geographical pattern of responses in timing and intensity of fluctuations.

Secondly, the assumption of homogeneous consumer demand, linked with elasticity, can also be abandoned, since there are noticeable variations in regional household expenditure. Regions are likely to transmit fluctuations more intensely if their marginal propensities to import goods forming a major part of their budget is high, and to be most vulnerable if such goods are a major part of their exports.

The third assumption to be dropped concerns the mobility of labour, the effect of whose disappearance is to exacerbate the employment problem found in highly specialized regions whose products are faced with high demand elasticities. Even in an economy where cyclical changes diffuse very rapidly it is unlikely that all industries and regions will react simultaneously but lack of occupational and industrial mobility tend to restrict the job-opportunity of those made unemployed. The position is likely to be eased only where there is a high density of employment with a large variety of industries, or where there is a subsistence sector (as in less developed countries) which can absorb additional labour.

Fourth, in reality regions contain a heterogeneous population and local variations occur in the age of population, and the sex and age composition of the workforce. For example, areas with a large retired component have a fairly stable volume of income from pensions, and a correspondingly low volume from regional trade, though this does not mean that they will not be vulnerable to fluctuations.

Fifth, by relinquishing perfect competition it becomes necessary to refer not only to industries but also to the firms which constitute them; that is, to recognise that variations occur within, as well as between, industries. Firms vary in their share of a market, and their profitability, and also in their capital equipment and managerial policy and skill. With such variations it is inevitable that the nature of firms found within a locality can provide a further source of disparity in regional responses to cycles: moreoever, it is one that is difficult to predict, though it is possible that in regions with larger populations of firms the special features of individual firms cancel out. In other regions (East Anglia, for example) it is common to find areas in which single firms dominate the local labour market. Moreover, these differ in their employment policies; some believe they should deliberately cushion the local economy as far as possible, while others appear to respond to cycles quickly and drastically.

Finally, substitution of demand for finished and unfinished goods and raw materials is mainly a long-term feature and, as such, not directly relevant to cyclical fluctuations, though a cycle may cause firms to alter long-term plans and thus influence their responses in subsequent cycles. It is on the consumer's side that substitution is more likely, and even here only where there are significant cross-elasticities of demand, such that reduction in income causes one product to be replaced by another in the consumer budget. However, the effect is likely to be as much between different qualities of the same item, as between dissimilar commodities, though both can have regional significance.

By removing all the assumptions contained in Table 2.1 the point is reached where theories become cumbersome and indeterminate as the number of supporting and counteracting variables is increased. Nevertheless, it is still possible to identify elements in the economic structure of regions which encourage geographically regular responses, though these may be masked to a greater or lesser extent by aspatial complexities. In the first category regions continue to possess spatial configurations in which different values can be attributed to places in them. Likewise, regions have hierarchical central place systems which may not closely resemble the theoretical economic landscape, but which still contain its major elements. Secondly, there are differences to be found in the industrial composition of areas.

Hypotheses and Variables

At the most simple level it is possible to formalize the relationship between amplitude and timing and these four factors in two linear equations. In the case of amplitudes this may be expressed as:

$$A_i = k - C_i - S_i + Y_i - (E_i - E_i^2) \quad \ldots\text{Equation 2}$$

where A is amplitude and the elements on the right of the equation are position in the central place hierarchy (C), measures of spatial structure (S), an indicator of the potential vulnerability of industrial composition (Y), and an element representing the growth in the area (E). The last item is written in a quadratic form to account for the possibility that areas with very high rates of growth might be exceptionally vulnerable to changes in investment and behave like areas with very slow growth or contraction. In any case, it is likely that increments to the rate of growth have a diminishing effect. The constant (k) can be interpreted as the share of the amplitude not attributable to geographical variations.

Timing is less readily reducible to a formal equation; as stated above, variations are more closely associated with the nature of the cycle and the vagaries of local responses. In addition, as many equations would be needed as there are turning points in a cycle. (In this study four are identified, at the start and end of each upswing and downswing, rather than just two, peaks and troughs, which are commonly found in other analyses). Nevertheless, if timing can be explained in terms of geographical factors then the expected relationships at 'beneficial' turning points would be:

$$Tb_i = k - C_i - S_i - Y_i - E_i \quad \ldots\text{Equation 3.}$$

That is, areas best located, with the most stable industrial compositions and fastest expansion would be the first to return to high levels of employment. At the detrimental turning points areas with the opposite characteristics would lead.

Each of these factors can be specified in a variety of independent variables. For example, spatial structure can be represented in many different ways and at different scales. Similarly, it is possible to define industrial composition by alternative measures, taking account of the entire range of activities in each area or concentrating on just the basic ones. Economic growth is even more elusive: it is arguable whether change in employment should be used, or change in output, and whether the current rate of development is more significant than the rate immediately past. Thus, in a sense, the variables described below are specified arbitrarily, though they are used only after some experiment with alternatives.

The hierarchy of centres in East Anglia has been defined in several studies and the pattern shown in Figure 2.5 has been derived from Smailes, [30] Smith, [31] and Carruthers. [32] Three main centres, Norwich, Ipswich and Southend, each with populations exceeding 100,000 dominated in the north, centre and south, respectively, of the region, although there are large interstices in East Anglia which lie outside their spheres of influence. The next rank consists of the subdominant centres, major market towns such as Colchester and Bury St. Edmunds, industrialized ports (Great Yarmouth and Lowestoft), King's Lynn, which combines the functions of port and market, Chelmsford, a largely industrialized market town and, by the end of the period, the two new towns (Harlow and Basildon). At subsequent levels, the lower ranks contain the small

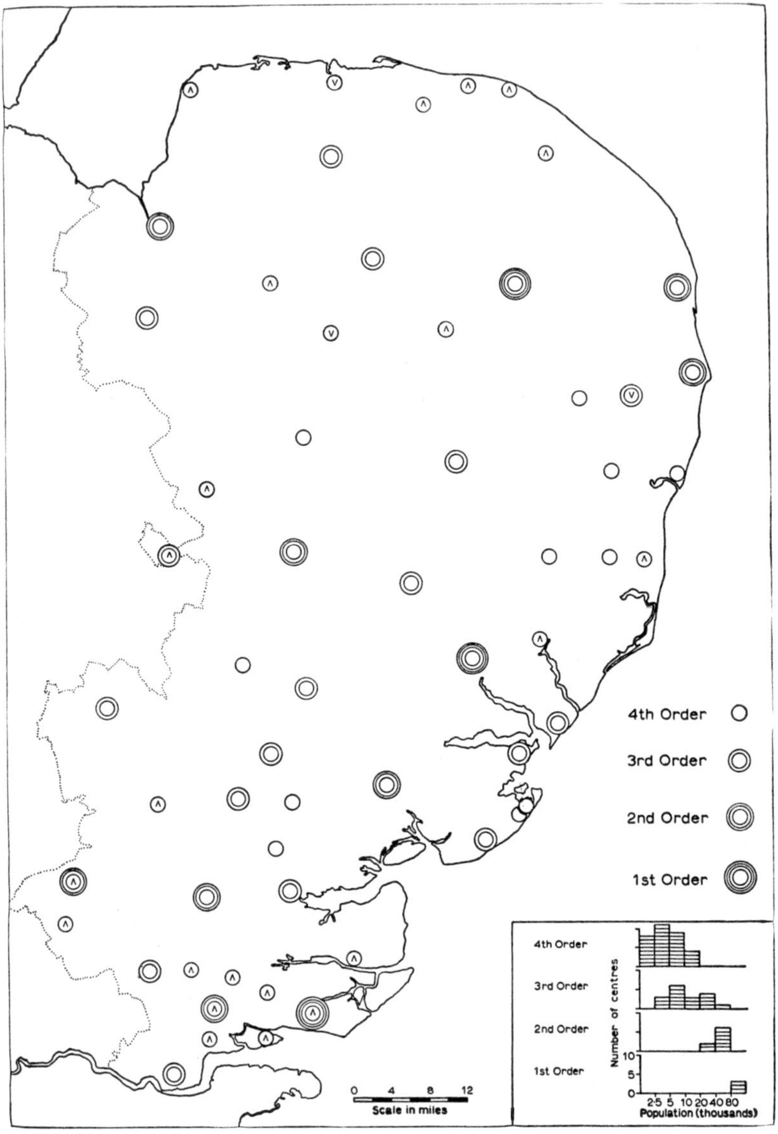

Figure 2.5. The hierarchy of settlements.
Promotion and relegation of settlements through the hierarchy is denoted by symbols Λ and V, respectively.

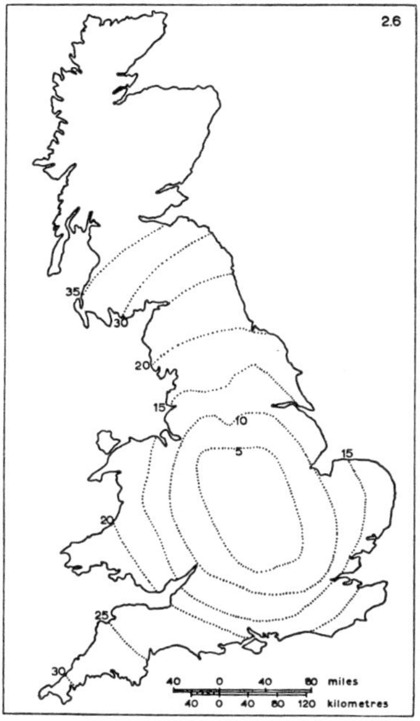

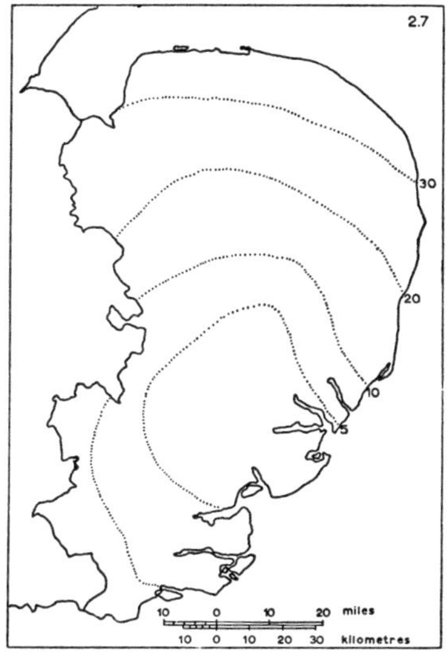

Figure 2.6. The Index of Location in Great Britain.

Figure 2.7. The Index of Location in East Anglia.

Figure 2.8. Local population potential in East Anglia (in 10,000's).

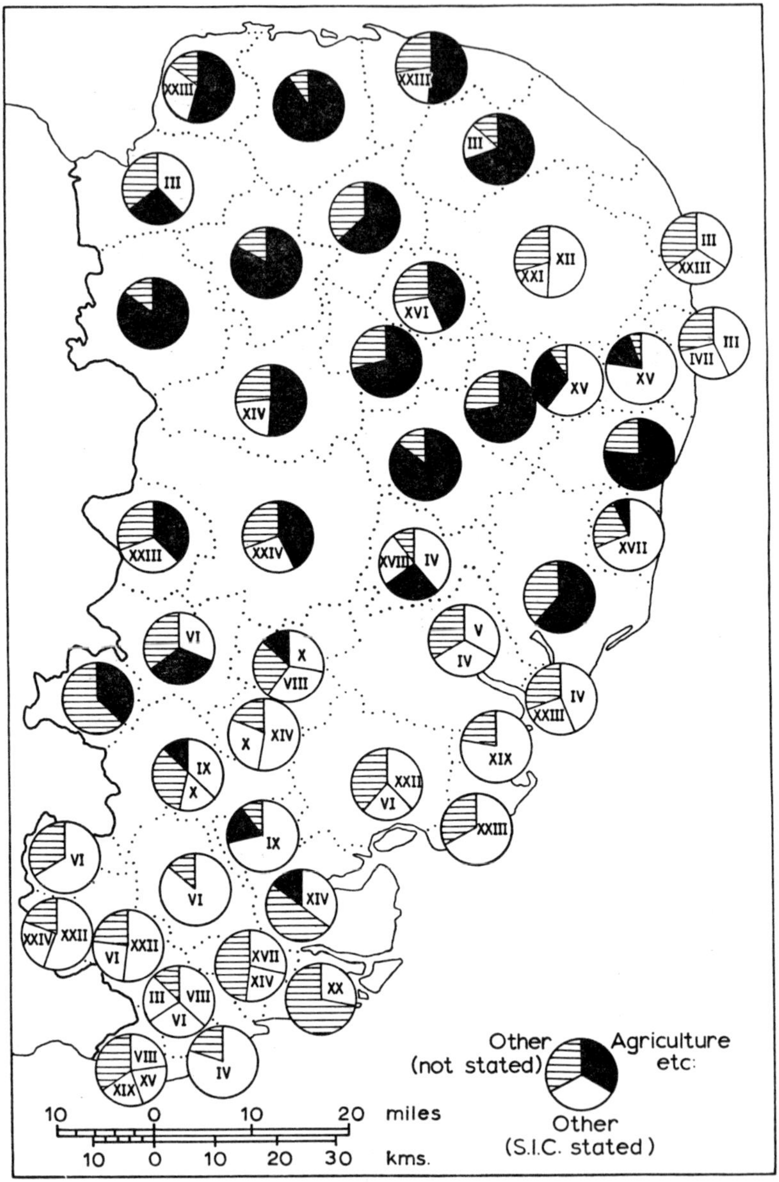

Figure 2.9. Principal Economic Bases, 1964.

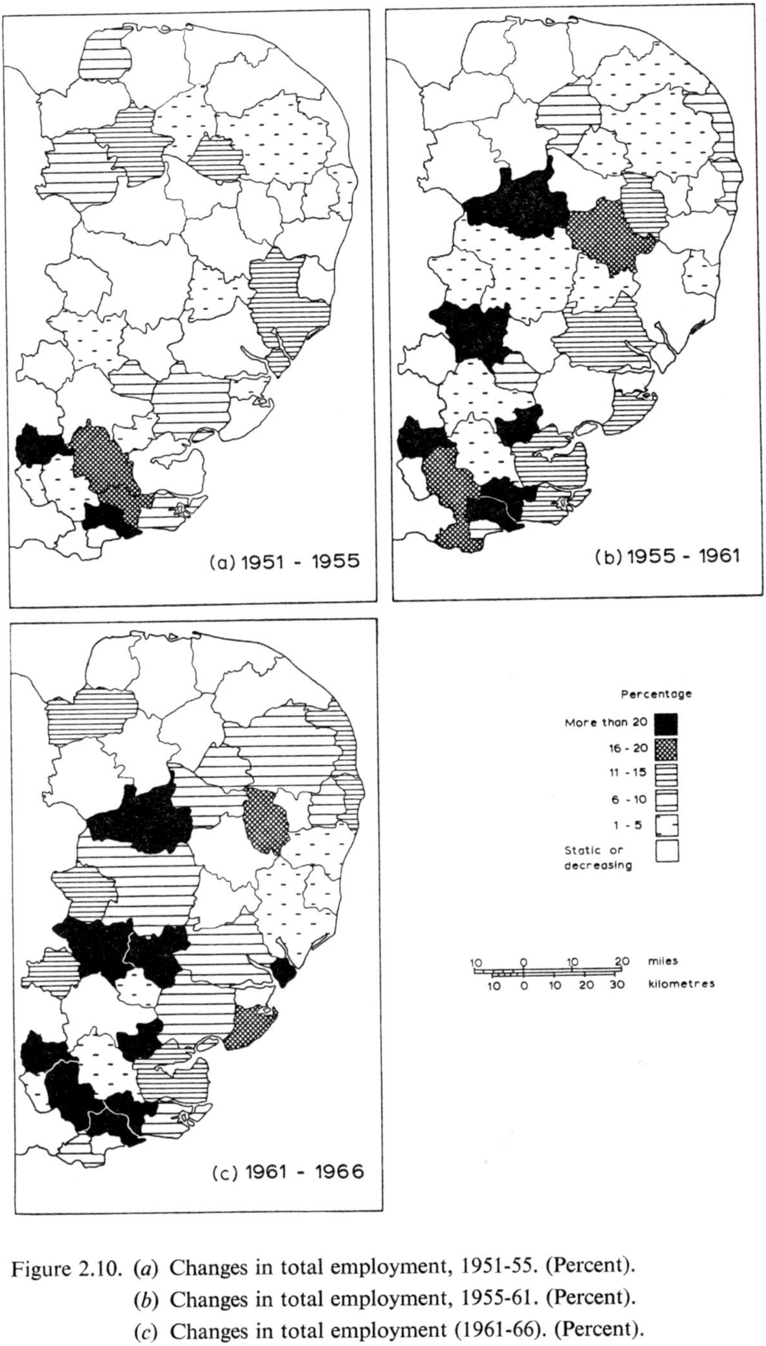

Figure 2.10. (*a*) Changes in total employment, 1951-55. (Percent).
(*b*) Changes in total employment, 1955-61. (Percent).
(*c*) Changes in total employment (1961-66). (Percent).

market towns, the majority of the region's coastal resorts, and the smaller industrial centres.

The region's spatial structure, defined here as a set of "potential" surfaces, is described at three separate scales. Using Dunn's index of location[33] values have been derived for sub-regions relative to the national population (Figure 2.6) and within the bounds of the region (Figure 2.7). Finally, local population fields (Figure 2.8) have been calculated by placing a 5-mile square grid over the region and summing the population in the four cells adjacent to each intersection.

In theory, the critical part of each area's industrial composition concerning the response to cyclical changes is the basic, or export, sector. A variety of techniques exist for identifying economic bases but the one adopted here is derived from Mattila and Thompson[34] and is related to the concept of the location quotient (and requires the same assumptions). That is, all industries with quotients greater than unity are basic industries, the difference between the quotient and unity being the basic component. This value can be translated into absolute numbers (of employees, in this case) and the numbers for all basic industries in an area summed to provide an estimate of the basic sector as a whole. Thereafter, the measure of industrial structure which is expected to explain cyclical vulnerability is taken as the proportion of the basic sector found in industries which have proved to be most volatile in their cyclical unemployment.[35] In Figure 2.9 the basic industries, but not their overall size, in each area are identified for a single year, 1964, although in the later analysis several years are used.

Changes in employment since 1951 are depicted in Figure 2.10. As a whole the rate of increase in the region was greater (by a factor of about 3.5) than in the whole country, but this was due largely to the development of the New Towns (from 1951), and town expansion schemes (from 1957). In addition, most of the southern parts of the region grew rapidly and there were some special cases, such as Great Yarmouth and Lowestoft which had a minor expansion in the early 1960's following the start of North Sea gas exploration. In contrast most of the rural northern part of the region lost employment or barely held constant.

References

1. Herschell, W. (1801). Observations tending to investigate the nature of the sun. *Philosophical Transactions*, 91, 265-318.
2. Kondratieff, N. D. (1935). The long waves in economic life. (trans. W. F. Stolper). *Review of Economics and Statistics*, 17, 105-115.
3. Parry Lewis, J. (1965). *Building Cycles and Britain's Growth*, London. Lösch, A. (1937). Population cycles as a cause of business cycles, *Quarterly Journal of Economics*, 51, 649-662.
4. Jevons, W. S. (1884). The periodicity of commercial crises and its physical explanation. Reprinted in (1953). *Readings in Business Cycles and National Income*, edited by Hansen, A. A. and R. V. Clemence (1953), pp. 83-95. London. A strong criticism of "sunspot" theories is contained in: Bryant, W. W. (1921) The Weather and cyclical fluctuations, *Economic Journal*, 31, 46-9.
5. Matthews, R. C. D. (1959) *The Trade Cycle*, London.

6. Abramoritz, M. (1950) *Inventories and Business Cycles, N.B.E.R.*, New York.
7. Jevons, W. S. (1884) Op. cit.
8. Habbakuk, H. J. (1962) Fluctuations in house building in Britain and the United States in the nineteenth century. *Journal of Economic History*, 22, p. 215.
9. Prest, A. R. ed. (1969) *The U.K. Economy: A Manual of Applied Economics*, London.
   Matthews, R. C. O. (1969) Postwar business cycles in the United Kingdom, in *Is The Business Cycle Obsolete?*, edited by M. Bronfenbrenner, pp. 99-135, New York.
10. Mitchell, W. C. (1951) *What Happens During Business Cycles, N.B.E.R.*, New York.
11. Mitchell, B. R. & P. Deane (1962) *Abstract of British Historical Statistics*, Cambridge.
12. Vining, R. (1945) Regional variations in cyclical fluctuations viewed as a frequency distribution, *Econometrica*, 13, 183-213.
13. Neff, P. (1949) Inter-regional variations in economic fluctuations. *American Economic Review*, 38, 105-119.
14. Kidner, F. L. (1949) Inter-regional variations in economic fluctuations. (Discussion) *American Economic Review*, 39, 127-130.
15. Keynes, J. M. (1936). *The General Theory of Employment, Interest and Money*, London.
16. Vining, R. (1946) The region as a concept in business cycle analysis, *Econometrica*, 14, 201-18.
17. Andrews, R. B. (1953-6) Mechanics of the urban economic base, *Land Economics*, vols. 29-31 (series of articles).
18. Demery, J. & F. Ritchie (1934) The westward lag in business. *Journal of Business*, 7, 173-181.
   Neff, P. & A. Weifenbach (1949) *Business Cycles in Selected Industrial Areas*. University of California Press, Berkeley.
   Williams, R. M. (1950) The timing and amplitude of regional business cycles. *Proc. of the 25th Annual Conference of Pacific Economic Association* pp. 47-50.
19. Vining, R. (1949) The region as an economic entity and certain variations to be observed in the study of systems of regions. *American Economic Review*, 39, 89-104.
20. Vining, R. (1946) op. cit.
21. Borts, G. (1960) Regional cycles of manufacturing employment in the United States, 1914-1953. *Journal of the American Statistical Association*, 55, 151-211.
22. Neff, P. (1949) op. cit. p. 117.
23. Vining, R. (1949) op. cit. pp. 102-3.
24. Harris, C. P. & A. P. Thirlwall (1968) Inter-regional variations in the cyclical sensitivity to unemployment in the U.K., 1949-1964. *Bulletin of the Oxford Institute of Economics and Statistics*, 30, 55-66.
25. Borts, G. (1960) op. cit. p. 180.
26. Steiner, R. L. (1949) Inter-regional variations in economic fluctuations. (Discussion) *American Economic Review*, 39, 130-34.
27. Nordling, C. O. (1967) Origin of a depression. *Land Economics*, 43, 64-70.
28. Lösch, A. (1954) *The Economics of Location*, Yale.
29. Berry, B. J. L. (1967) *Geography of Market Centres and Retail Distribution*. New Jersey, 93-114.
30. Smailes, A. E. (1944) The urban hierarchy in England and Wales, *Geography*, 36, 41-51.
31. Smith, R. D. P. (1968) The changing urban hierarchy, *Regional Studies*, 2, 1-19.

32. Carruthers, W. I. (1967) Major shopping centres in England and Wales, *Regional Studies,* 1, 65-81.
33. Dunn, E. S. (1956) The market potential concept and the analysis of location. *Papers and Proceedings of the Regional Science Association,* 2, 183-194.
34. Mattila, J. M. and W. R. Thompson (1955). Measurement of the economic base of the Metropolitan area. *Land Economics,* 31, 215-228.
35. In Great Britain between 1951 and 1966 varied from 0·3% to 2·6% for different industries, with a slight break in the range at about 0·7%. The stable group comprises Professional Services (SIC XXII), Mining and Quarrying (II), Insurance, etc. (XXI), Gas, etc. (XVIII), Paper, etc. (XV), Vehicles (VIII), Public administration (XXIV), Chemicals (IV), Transport (XIX), and Engineering (VI). The unstable group contains: Agriculture, etc. (I), Distributive Trades (XX), Metal Manufactures (V and IX), Textiles (X), Food, etc. (III), Other Manufacturing (XVI), Leather Goods (XI), Timber, etc. (XIV), Bricks, etc. (XIII), Clothing & Footwear (XII), Miscellaneous Services (XXIII), Shipbuilding (VII) and Construction (XVII). 1958 Standard Industrial Classification.

III

Components of Unemployment Patterns: 1951-1968

Local cycles occur within two broader contexts: first, they are part of the cycle taking place within a larger area (the region or the nation); second, they occur simultaneously with a number of other economic changes. Examination of these milieux accounts for the greater part of the present chapter. Cycles in East Anglia and Great Britain are identified first; there then follows a discussion of problems and techniques in the analysis of time series, prior to an investigation of aggregative variations among the components of unemployment which include non-cyclical, as well as cyclical, changes.

Cycles in East Anglia and Great Britain, 1951-68

Table 3.1 Timing and amplitude in regional and national unemployment cycles (seasonally adjusted), 1951-68.

	East Anglia		Great Britain	
Phase	Date	% unemp't	Date	% unemp't
Trough	Aug 51	·9	Aug. 51	1·6
Peak	Dec. 52	2·1	Nov. 52	2·5
Trough	Oct. 55	1·1	Dec. 55	1·4
Peak	May 58	2·8	Nov. 58	3·3
Trough	Feb. 61	1·6	Feb. 61	2·0
Peak	Feb. 63	2·7	Mar. 63	3·6
Trough	Feb. 66	1·5	Mar. 66	1·8
Peak	?	?	?	?

Sources: (*a*) East Anglia; unpublished tabulations. (*b*) Great Britain; Ministry of Labour Gazette.

Note: East Anglian data for males only; G.B. is for males and females.

The regional and national series both contained three complete major cycles in unemployment, with peaks in 1952, 1958 and 1963. (Table 3.1). An additional recession, with a minor peak, occurred in 1956-57 (associated with a series of minor crises) but it lacked the general impact exhibited in the others and forms part of the upswing leading to the 1958 peak. After 1963 unemployment fell until 1966, when a new upswing began, the end of which occurred after the close of this time series.

Figure 3.1. Employment exchange areas in East Anglia

Similarities between the three main cycles occurred in their periodicity and amplitude. Equivalent phases occurred at intervals of between 50 and 65 months in the regional series, and amplitudes were between 1% and 1·2% (with one exception); in Great Britain periodicities were about the same, but amplitudes slightly higher. However, no two cycles were identical, although all were associated with the same general set of causes. Moreover, cycles took place against a background of economic growth, which, being unevenly distributed (regionally and sectorally), ensured that each cycle functioned differently. Added to this, cyclical forces were opposed by different economic policies at different times. In the 1950's and early 1960's monetary measures tended to be used most, leading to more diffuse regional responses. Greater emphasis was placed on direct measures after 1964, and those used in mid-1966 to secure deflation had more immediate impact.

Analysis of Time Series

The unemployment numbers which comprise the basic set of data relate to all 45 employment exchange areas (Figure 3.1) for each month between March 1951 and February 1968; this period was the limit for a continuous series at the time of collection. These were then divided by the annual estimates of total employees to provide estimated rates of unemployment.

In the identification of cyclical fluctuations from a basic set of unemployment series three alternative strategies can be used. First, the data can be left in its unadjusted state, but this is unsatisfactory since cyclical parameters may be hidden by other components (seasonal, trend, and random). Second, it is possible to subject the unadjusted series to spectral analysis,[1] in which the objective is to find a function which describes the oscillatory nature of the series. However, although this is a most valuable technique for identifying periodicities in fluctuations in very long and complicated series it does not preserve sufficient of the original series and is less valuable for detailed analysis of the sequence of events in a series. Thus, the third alternative, seasonal adjustment is preferred.

Seasonal adjustment is a common procedure, but one for which there is no universally accepted method.[2] The most economical, but potentially inaccurate, is to rely upon the values for only a single month in each year; usually a summer month when demand for labour is at its seasonal peak. Although often used, it is clear that by ignoring the remaining eleven months there are dangers of overlooking the real timing and amplitudes of a cycle. An improvement on this is to calculate a moving average (method 1) consisting of one summer and one winter value (separated by six months, for example July and January). This is more sensitive to changes, but like the first method may suppress the extreme movements and cause some difficulty in the identification of turning points. However, it does produce a smooth graph of the series, and for this reason is adopted as one of the two adjustment techniques used in this study. The graphs in Figure 3.2 (*b*) are derived from July/January moving averages for Norwich.

To supplement this a more precise form of adjustment (method 2), based on a multiplicative calculation[3] is used: basically, values for

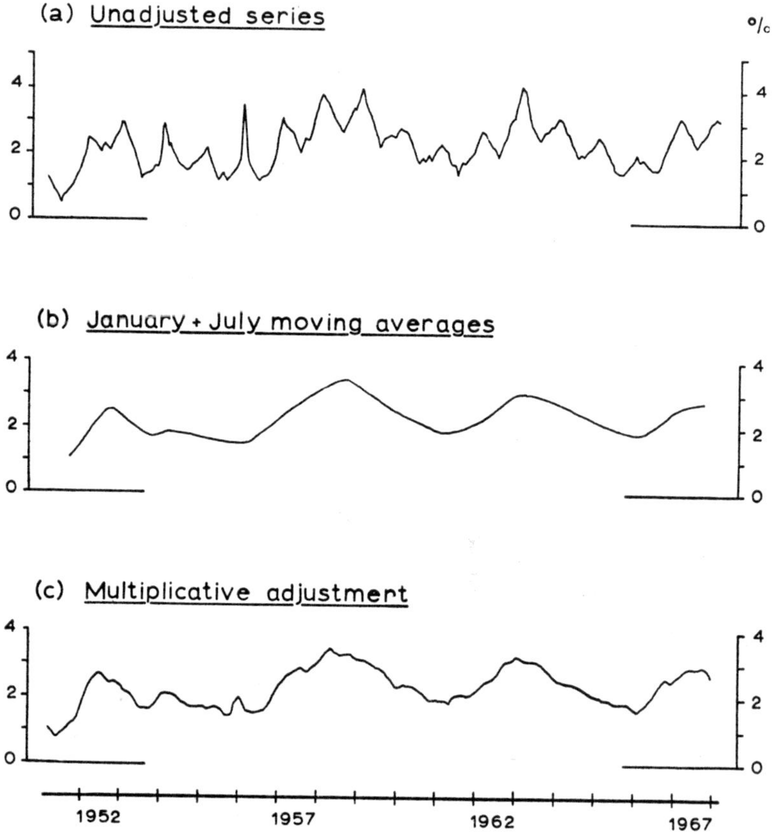

Figure 3.2. Unemployment in Norwich, 1951-1968: alternative methods of adjustment in time series.

equivalent months of each year are compared with their average. To calculate such a seasonal adjustment the following equation is used:

$$M_{ai} = M_{ui} * \frac{M_a}{A_t}$$

where M_{ai} is the seasonally adjusted value of month $_a$ in year $_i$

M_{ui} is the unadjusted value of month $_a$ in year $_i$

M_a is the unadjusted mean value for month $_a$

and A_t is the mean of all months.

Thus each month is given a weighting (M_a/A_t) which, when multiplied by the basic figures (M_{ui}) produces an adjusted value. A further modification can be made to remove some smaller irregularities by applying a three-month moving average which helps to dampen any brief anomalies caused by abnormal climatic conditions or occasional inaccuracies in reported unemployment.

No other adjustments have been carried out on these series, although there is a case to be made for trend adjustments. However, with only a few exceptions there was no marked trend in unemployment in East Anglia, and it was decided to leave the series to indicate trends wherever they occurred, since it was commonly found that trends and cycles were closely related. That is, accelerations in trend coincided with upswings in the cycle and failure to return to previous low levels of unemployment.

Cyclical Components

Having adjusted all the series to remove seasonal effects attention can be concentrated on the three main cyclical features: amplitude, timing and conformity. Graphs of the series adjusted by method 1 are presented in Figure 3.3. These are arranged on the basis of a cluster analysis (described below) carried out to definite business cycle regions and inserted with each group are (i) the turning points in the regional series and each local series, and (ii) the level of correlation between local and regional series.

The timing of cyclical changes. The most challenging problem in business cycle studies (whether of regions or economic sectors) is the identification and explanation of the timing and order in which responses occur. If patterns are repeated through a series of cycles their identification allows future cyclical movements to be predicted with some confidence. This has been the general principle behind the study of business indicators, resulting in the recognition of a diffusion process through large numbers of sectors.[4] The basis for such analysis is the notion that general cycles are the aggregate of many separate series, (in the case of the East Anglian cycle, of its 45 areas), and there tends to be a considerable range around the regional value for any parameter. (Figure 3.4).

Moreover, the pattern which emerges when the frequency distribution is compared with the regional series is clear. As a general observation, the form of regional series is dependent upon the balance between areas with increasing and decreasing cyclical unemployment, but there is a lag

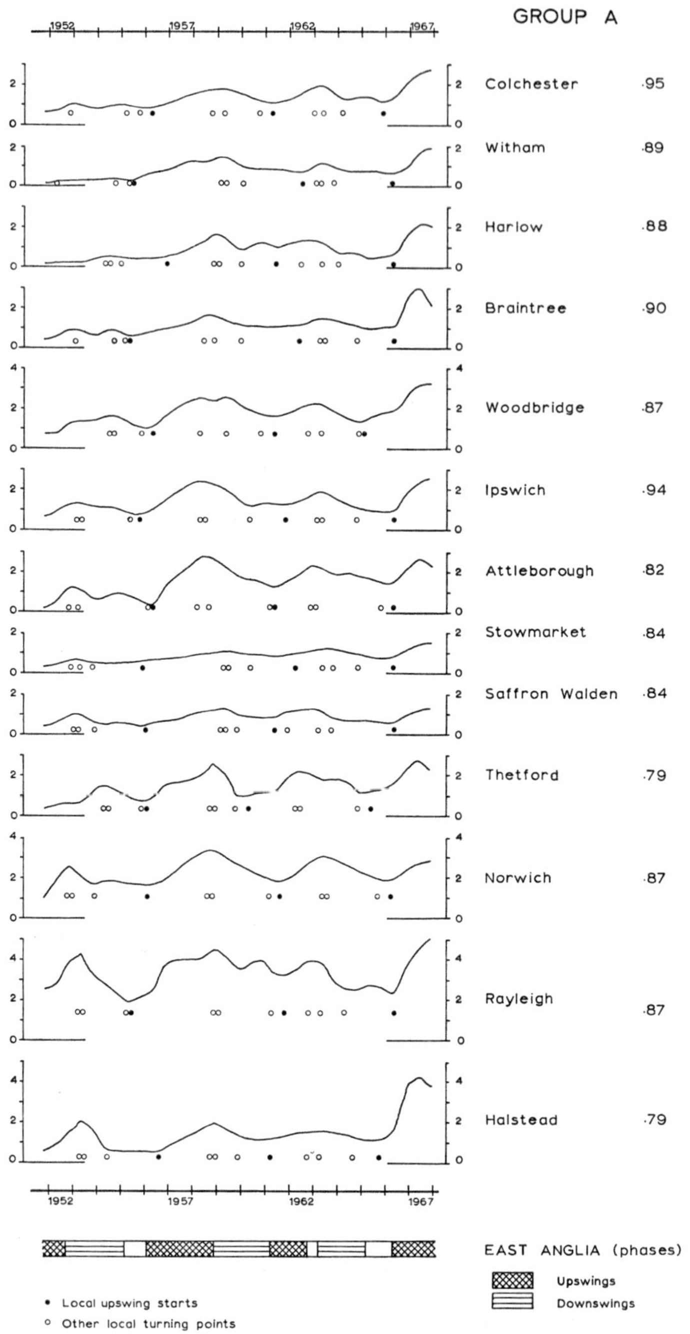

Figure 3.3. Seasonally adjusted unemployment series, by exchange area, 1951-68. Figures to the right of graphs refer to index of conformitv.

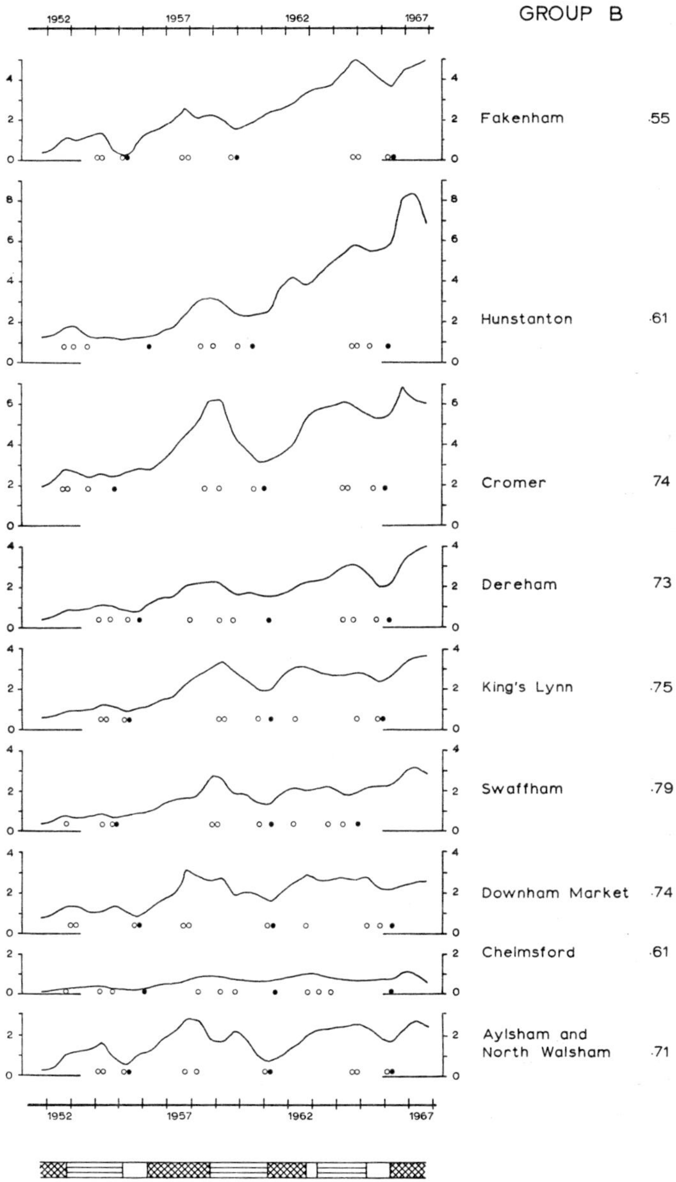

Figure 3.3—(*continued*)

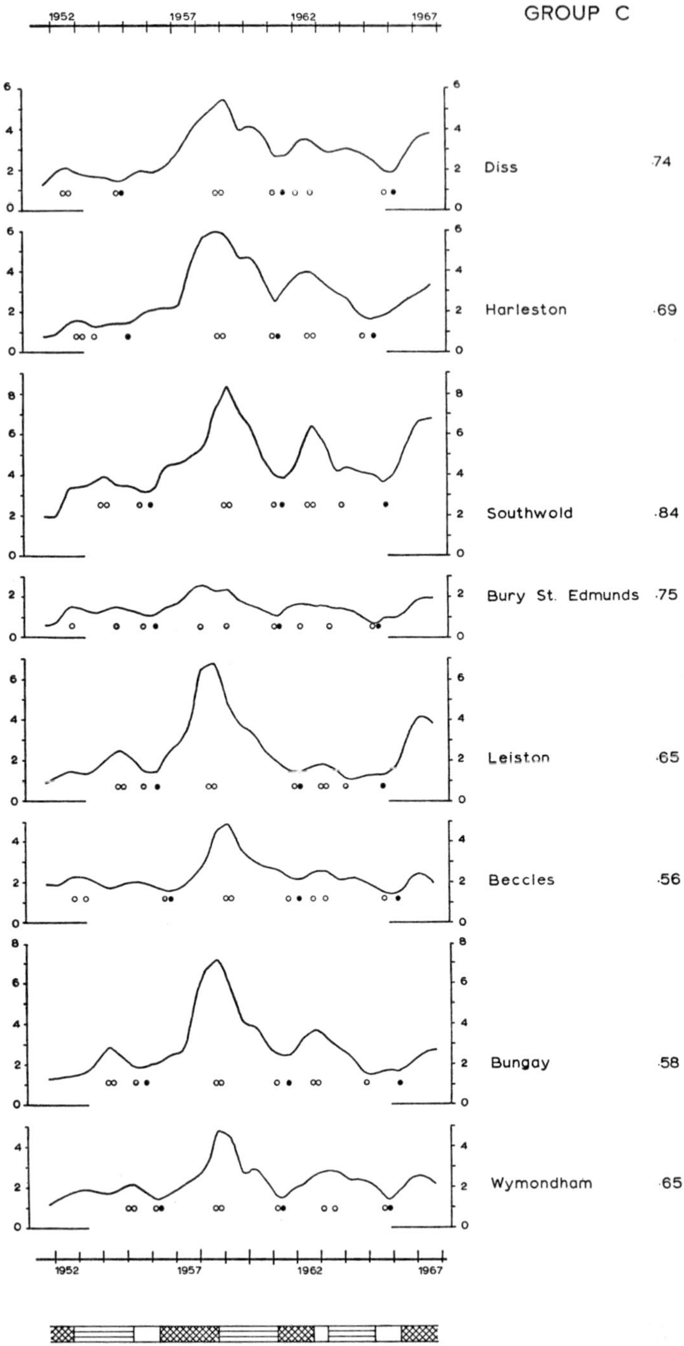

Figure 3·3—(*continued*)

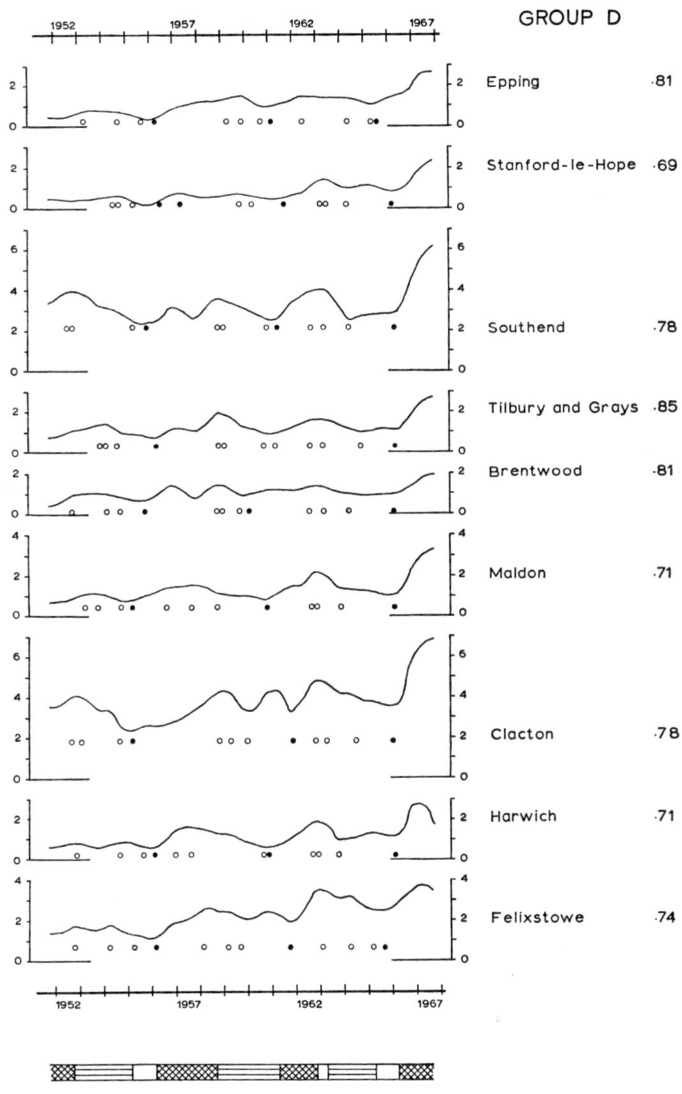

Figure 3·3—(*continued*)

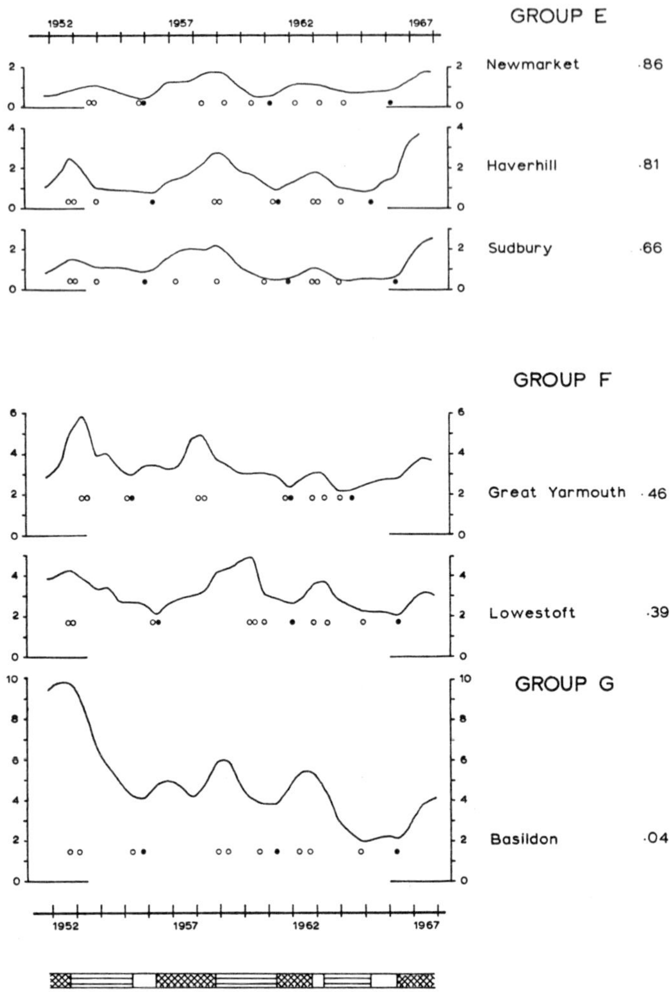

Figure 3·3—(*continued*)

effect. The maximum numbers of increases occurred early in the upswing, followed by the maxima of "no changes" at the peak in unemployment. There was then a rapid shift to maximum numbers of areas with decreases, the number falling as the trough was approached. Finally, the trough itself was marked by large numbers with "no change", as at the peak. The overall result is similar to Vining's description of the frequency distribution in American cycles.[5]

The problem of identifying the timing of cyclical movements in local series can be approached through three alternative methods: namely, series inter-correlation, peak and trough dating, and turning point dating. The first is based on the premise that timing should be measured along

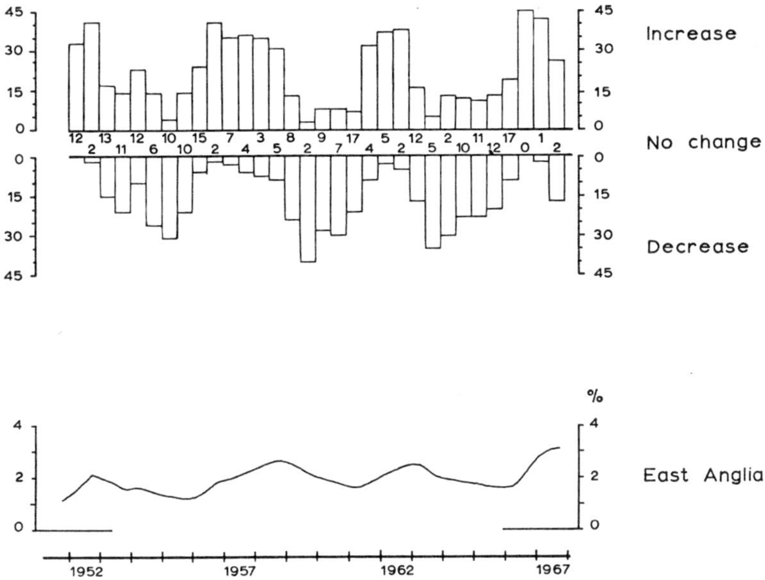

Figure 3.4. Frequency distributions of movements in the seasonally adjusted unemployment series.

the whole of the series, rather than at specific points, to take account of the form of cyclical shifts; for example, whether upswings or downswings are convex or concave. Its method is a lengthy procedure of iterative correlations with an incremental lag at each stage, using either an n(n-1) matrix (each area being lagged against every other), or an $n \times 1$ vector (each area being lagged against a reference series). The highest correlation denotes the amount of lag (which may be zero) that produces the "best fit" between any pair of series. Although used with apparent success in the Mid-West of the United States in an analysis of a single upswing,[6] experiment with a long, complex, series shows the technique to be vulnerable to short, random, movements leading to spurious correlations. More important, it ignores the actual turning points, which reduces its value considerably. This deficiency is partly met by the second method, dating the peaks and troughs in the series. However, this also is unsatisfactory, not only because such points are often impossible to identify (frequently one finds "plateaux" and "plains" rather than peaks and troughs) but also because it is more logical to consider cycles to have four turning points rather than two. That is, instead of a sudden reversal in cyclical series, it is normal to find changes in direction at the beginning and end of each upswing and downswing. These may coincide, but more often the start of an upswing follows a period of low unemployment existing since the end of the previous downswing; the end of the upswing is then likely to be followed by a period of high, possibly stable, unemployment. Thus the third approach is adopted here, with the turning points assessed from the graphs in Figure 3.3.

Table 3.2. Frequency distribution of turning points, 1951-67

		– Number of areas –			
		– upswing –		– downswing –	
	Date	start	stop	start	stop
1	July 51/Jan 52				
2	Jan 52/July 52		4		
3	July 52/Jan 53		19	9	
4	Jan 53/July 53		11	12	
5	July 53/Jan 54		1	2	8
6	Jan 54/July 54		9	12	1
7	July 54/Jan 55	3	1	8	7
8	Jan 55/July 55	10		2	15
9	July 55/Jan 56	10			11
10	Jan 56/July 56	19			2
11	July 56/Jan 57	2	2		
12	Jan 57/July 57	1	2		
13	July 57/Jan 58		4	4	
14	Jan 58/July 58		8	3	1
15	July 58/Jan 59		20	19	1
16	Jan 59/July 59		8	16	
17	July 59/Jan 60	1		2	12
18	Jan 60/July 60	2	1	1	6
19	July 60/Jan 61	3			11
20	Jan 61/July 61	21			12
21	July 61/Jan 62	13	2		2
22	Jan 62/July 62	5	9	1	1
23	July 62/Jan 63		21	10	
24	Jan 63/July 63		8	23	
25	July 63/Jan 64		2	3	10
26	Jan 64/July 64	1	3	2	8
27	July 64/Jan 65	2		5	10
28	Jan 65/July 65	5		1	7
29	July 65/Jan 66	7			9
30	Jan 66/July 66	30			1
31	July 66/Jan 67				
32	Jan 67/July 67				

Note: Movements in 1952 based on estimates, since previous unemployment levels were unknown

By abstracting the turning points from each area's series and combining them to form the sequential frequency distribution in Table 3.2 it can be seen that at each phase there occurred a range of changes, usually distributed with some skewness about the mean date. The only major deviation occurred in 1966 when strong deflationary measures caused a large number of areas, thereto showing high demand for labour, to respond together. An indication of the degree of conformity between areas is found in the relatively small amount of overlap between different phases in the cycles. This was greatest, as might be expected, between the end of one movement (up or down) and the start of the next: it was rare for any area to have completed an upswing (or downswing) before others had ended their downswing (or upswing).

This is important, for it denotes that while there were significant variations in timing, these were not so great as would have occurred if each series had followed a random course. In effect they validate the whole of the ensuing analysis.

The distribution in Table 3.2 can also be investigated for its geographical patterns. To do this the twelve turning points are divided into their four components, every area thus having three values for each component. At each of these it is noted whether, relative to the median group, an area led, lagged or conformed. Where at least two of the three readings were the same the area was attributed that characteristic for the component. However, for the purpose of Figure 3.5 areas with median timing are grouped with those which led.

In theoretical statements the relative position of an area's turning points is dependent upon the transmission process operating through its industrial composition. However, these tend to be made in aggregative terms (for example, that demand for investment goods is most volatile, followed by consumer durables) and impossible to verify satisfactorily using the Standard Industrial Classification which does not distinguish between the sectoral destinations of industrial output. This has compounded the problems of explaining identified differences in timing, adding to the difficulties caused by generally weak evidence. Thus the imperfect patterns of Figure 3.5 are partly expected. At all four stages areas with similar turning points are found to have different explanations for their behaviour, and there was considerable intermixture of areas with different timing.

Assuming that unemployment has been low and stable, the beginning of an upswing can be either a gradual process, with areas becoming affected over a long period (as in the first two cycles), or be relatively sharp (as in 1966, when the remaining two-thirds of the areas were all affected by the deflationary measures). Of all the turning points this is the one most influenced by economic policies and decisions. Yet the pattern in Figure 3.5a shows some geographical differentiation. The leading group was predominantly rural, but included areas with manufacturing and service bases (two of which, Great Yarmouth and Southend, were also major urban areas). With the exception of the last two areas the common factors were their low employment densities and relatively slow growth which, added to their agricultural bases, gave rise to few alternative job opportunities. Most were also areas with above average unemployment, where there would be a lower incidence of labour hoarding, and effective demand for labour would respond more rapidly to changes in economic conditions. In addition, the northern areas (including Great Yarmouth) had low regional and national indices of location which, in theory, made them more vulnerable to falling demand in competition with areas more favourably located. Finally, manufacturing bases appear to have had some relevance. Maldon and Halstead both had major proportions of their employment in the manufacture of constructional timber, which tends to be affected rapidly when industrial and residential building (themselves volatile) contract or even slow down their rate of expansion: in an accelerator model suppliers of intermediate goods are affected more markedly (even if not more rapidly) than suppliers

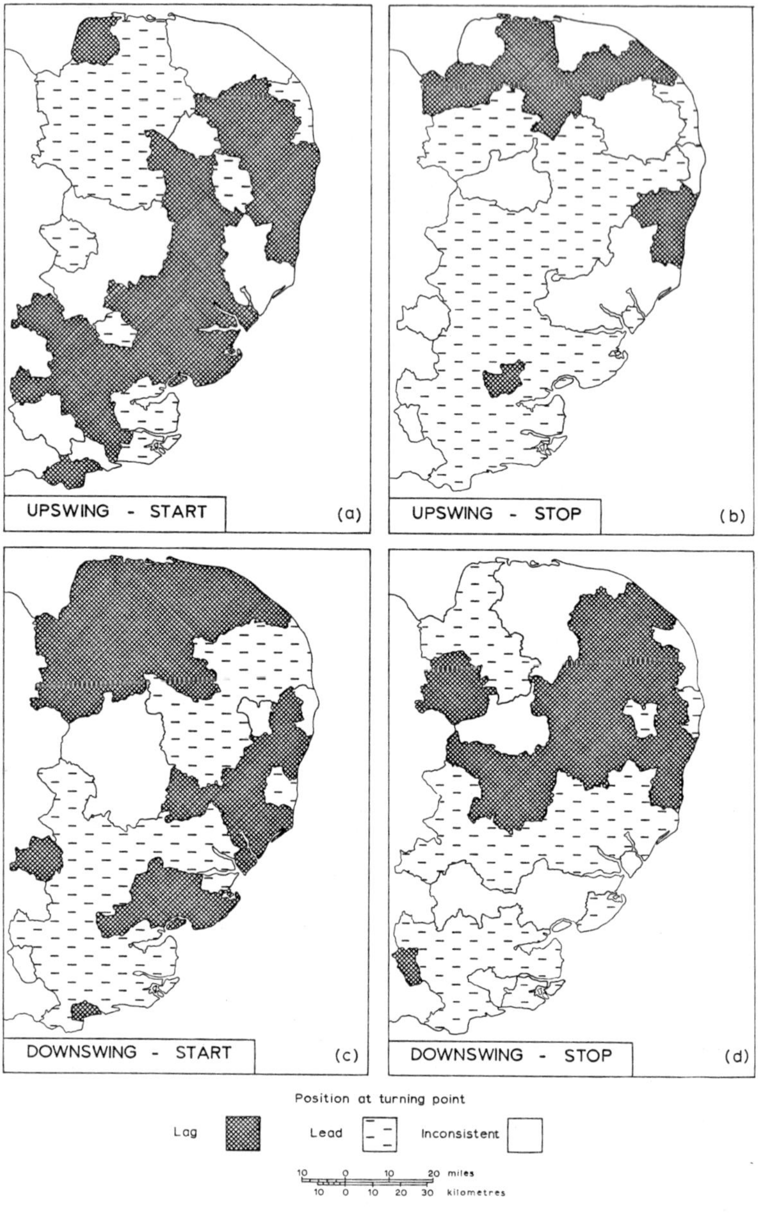

Figure 3.5 Timing of cyclical turning points, by exchange area. Distributions are based on three complete cycles.

of final goods, and in construction the intermediate functions tend to be more concentrated geographically. In Southend and Great Yarmouth the role of manufacturing is less easily explained, but both had significant employment in durable goods manufacture (electrical equipment) which, in theory, tend to lead, although other areas with similar bases showed opposite timing. Indeed, with these two exceptions, and Brentwood (which was inconsistent), all the major urban-industrial areas lagged, supporting the contention that in timing the pattern at this micro-geographical level, at least, is determined less by the conventional division between durable and non-durable goods manufacture than by the density of job opportunities (seen partly in average rates of unemployment) regardless of what the jobs might be.

The end of the upswing (Figure 3.5b) shows a general reversal of the pattern. Lagging areas now tended to be those with weak underlying growth trends (with the exception of Witham) and low employment densities. Thus most of rural north Norfolk and part of north east Suffolk tended to continue increasing after others had stopped. The industrial members at the start of the upswing, however, were leaders also at the end. An explanation is that at this stage employment in their industries was stabilized as demand for construction and durable goods stopped falling, although this leaves Witham, with a heavy dependence on metal constructional fitments in an anomalous position.

A much clearer pattern occurred at the start of the downswing (Figure 3.5c), when expansionary forces work most strongly, and changes take place in an economic environment relatively free from government intervention, in contrast to the start of the upswing. Here the differentiation was most marked between rural-agricultural and urban-industrial areas, with little overlap. Apparently, the resumption of growing demand had a faster impact on areas for whose products the marginal propensity to consume was highest, but this is not the sole factor. The probability of finding employment varies with the density of opportunities, and also with the degree of specialization in an area. In the latter case areas with only a single major industry (especially if contained in a single firm) might undergo a major reorganization of production, leading to a lower demand for labour. This appeared most strikingly at Stanford-le-Hope, where successive productivity increases in oil refining delayed the start of downswings in its unemployment series, but appeared also in several market towns similarly dominated, such as Wymondham, Stowmarket and Beccles.

Finally, the end of the downswing (Figure 3.5d) presents the most variegated pattern, due to alternative interpretations which can be placed on turning points at this stage. An early end to the downswing can be due either to a rapid return to low unemployment levels, or to a weak local economy prematurely terminating the cyclical improvement. Thus the leading group contained both categories, with the latter represented in northwest Norfolk. While it is similarly possible for lagging areas to contain those whose underlying growth trend continues to bring down unemployment this was a category not represented in East Anglia. Instead, most were associated with slower rates of growth and low job densities making placement of unemployed in jobs a lengthier process, and causing these areas to reach their peak employment at later dates.

Levels of conformity. A problem which emerges from the preceding section is that areas responded in different ways. In relation to the regional series there were variations between areas, and also within areas between cycles. This leads to questions about the degree of conformity occurring over the region. How closely did areas match the regional series? What was the effect in different cycles? Which areas conformed closely, and which badly?

For the measurement of conformity the method adopted is an unlagged correlation of the specific series, derived from multiplicative adjustment, with the regional series. The result is a set of coefficients within the usual bounds (plus and minus unity), with high positive scores indicating high conformity in timing and trend. In general the problem of autocorrelation in time series analysis means that the results of such a method have to be treated with care, since higher than usual coefficients are expected and it is possible also for short-lived random movements to upset the coefficients considerably. Nevertheless, for levels of conformity the technique allows more rigorous measurements than any other.

First, a comparison of conformity in the three separate cycles and the complete series is made in Table 3.3, in which the median, quartile and extreme coefficients are identified. In every cycle, and over the whole series there were always areas which clearly did not conform, failing even to surpass the normal product moment correlation coefficient necessary for significant association at the 95% confidence level. However, such areas were always a small minority. There was also a strong distinction between the first and the two last cycles indicating a positive correlation between the level of conformity and the severity of a cycle. The first cycle, occurring in a period of readjustment in the post-war economy (including planned industrial movements) and having a smaller rise in unemployment, had the least homogeneous set of responses. The others might have had even higher coefficients but for variations in response to the complex 1956-58 recession, and strong adverse trends in north Norfolk, especially after 1960.

Table 3.3 Levels of conformity between specific cycles and the reference cycle

	Aug 51/ Sept 55	Oct. 55/ Jan 61	Feb. 61/ Jan 66	April 51/ Jan 68
Maximum	·93	·98	·95	·95
Upper decile	·75	·91	·90	·88
Upper quartile	·62	·87	·85	·84
Median	·45	·79	·70	·75
Lower quartile	·31	·72	·60	·66
Lower decile	·19	·59	·39	·55
Minimum	·03	·07	·01	·04
coefficient for 99% signif.	·35	·31	·33	·18
number of months	50	64	60	202

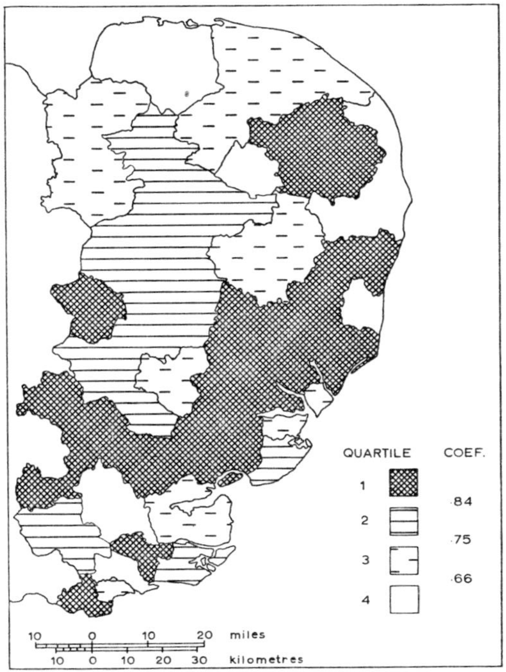

Figure 3.6. Conformity in cyclical behaviour, by exchange area

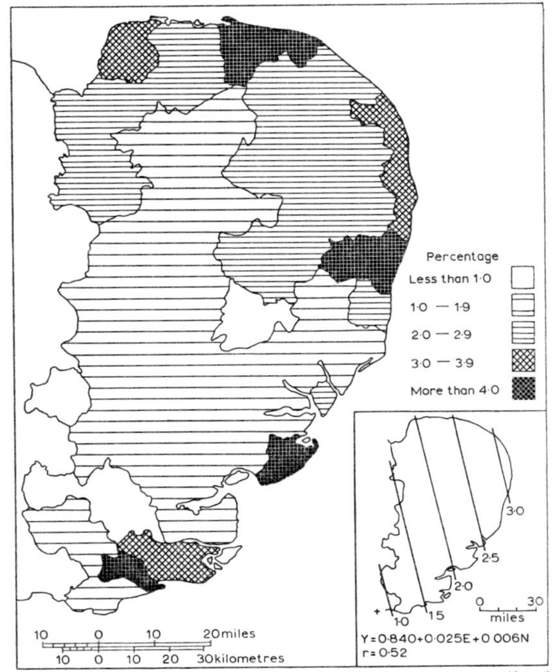

Figure 3.7 Cyclical unemployment in East Anglia; average amplitude, 1951-1966. The calculation is based on movements experienced in the three complete cycles occurring in the period. [Inset: linear trend surface for average amplitudes].

Secondly, when the overall levels of conformity found in individual areas are identified in Figure 3.6 groups with different characteristics are formed. Areas with median locations tended to conform well with the reference series, which is itself approximately a median series. However, more than this was required for good conformity, and these areas were associated also with moderate rates of growth and industrial diversification. That is, they resembled the regional "profile" in most of its features more closely than did areas in the lower quartiles. Lower levels, on the other hand, tended to be associated with a variety of extremes. Basildon, with the fastest growth in the region, had the lowest coefficient; Harlow, though conforming well overall, started badly at a time when it, too, was growing most rapidly. Lowestoft and Great Yarmouth both had strong improvements in their unemployment trends, associated with industrial development. At the other extreme, areas in north Norfolk, the region's main "problem" area, had low coefficients as a result of their weak growth leading to very small downswings at the end of each cycle. A number of highly specialised areas were also included. Two, Chelmsford and Stanford-le-Hope, had very low average unemployment rates, associated with their heavy concentration on electrical engineering and oil refining (making them the two most specialised areas in the region), and their unemployment series showed barely any response to changes in demand. However, their low conformity was due less to this than to a slight (and in realistic terms quite unimportant) upward trend in unemployment. High specialization was also a feature of parts of northeast Suffolk, and Leiston, Beccles and Bungay were also found in the lowest quartile. In all three cases their series indicate massive increases in cycle amplitude between 1955 and 1961 (sufficient except in the case of Beccles to become DATAC areas) followed by a return to very low amplitudes and improving trends in the 1961-1966 cycle. In the case of Leiston the latter period coincides with extra demand for labour created in the construction of a nuclear power station.

Levels of conformity, therefore, were relatively high: and would have been higher if specific series had been lagged against the regional series, since some series exhibited consistent deviations in timing. However, the latter course would provide only a marginal improvement at the cost of a more informative picture from the unlagged series, which indicates how closely, over specified periods, different areas respond to the same changes in the economic environment.

Cycle amplitudes. Although it is only one of the important features in cycle studies, amplitude tends to be given most attention, because it is the only one which contributes to the formation of economic policies. Upswings in unemployment series mean not only a reduction in utilized capacity but also considerable distress for those affected, prompting remedial action in the form of social security payments and regional economic policy. In addition it is the cyclical parameter which is most easily explained, although most explanations of it have been based on inter-industrial factors and tended to treat intra-industrial factors too superficially.

Measurement of cycle amplitudes requires only a comparison of maximum and minimum values occurring in each cycle in the multiplicatively adjusted series. The six values derived from measurements of upswing and downswings (ignoring the 1966 upswing) can then be treated individually, as in Chapter 4, averaged over each cycle (measured from trough to trough), or averaged over the whole period (1951-1966) as in Figure 3.7 to provide a general appreciation of cycle amplitudes. It can be anticipated, however, that each cycle showed a marginally different set of responses from its predecessor, as cycles themselves varied and as the regional economy underwent changes. An indication of the amount of difference between the average amplitudes of the three cycles is contained in Table 3.4, in the form of rank correlation coefficients.

Table 3.4 Rank order correlation coefficients of amplitudes, 1951-1966. 45 areas

	1951-1955	1955-1961	1961-1966
1951-1955	1·0		
1955-1961	0·77	1·0	
1961-1966	0·58	0·63	1·0

Average amplitudes varied considerably, from about 0·5% in Chelmsford to over 3·5% in Southwold, and the distribution over the entire range of values was positively skewed. A comparison of the extreme cases tends to lead to an explanation based on inter-industrial factors for the two groups were significantly different in their compositions. Small cyclical amplitudes were associated in general with basic sectors in engineering (especially electrical), and chemicals; large ones with resorts and agriculture. However, this leaves several anomalies, in addition to the mass of areas found between the extremes, for which industrial composition offers a barely acceptable explanation. This implies a need for at least a multivariate approach in order to evaluate the weight of intra- as well as inter-industrial factors; this is carried out in detail in Chapter 4, but the pattern in Figure 5.9 suggests factors, additional to industrial composition, which contribute something to its explanation.

First, there is a problem concerning amplitudes in rural areas, which tended to be only slightly less high than in resorts. Although largely attributable to fluctuations in agricultural employment, this is not an industry which might be expected to respond markedly to cyclical forces, as a producer of goods for which income elasticity tends to be low. In addition it might be expected that changes in interest rates and liquidity would make it more difficult to substitute machinery for manpower. It appears more valid, therefore, to seek an explanation in the nature of rural areas, in addition to their agricultural bases. These are areas of low earnings and low job densities providing few alternative opportunities within a short commuting distance. Combining these two factors, it is probable that, once out of work, the drop in income to the level of unemployment benefits is less drastic than for higher paid urban workers, and the lack of local opportunities reduces the chance of finding a new job.

Second there appeared to be a significant spatial component, summarised in a linear trend surface which alone accounted for over 25% of the regional variance. This, dipping north-eastwards, approximated the combined effects of regional and national locational indices, and cut across areas which, in terms of cycle amplitudes, had similar industrial compositions. As with timing, the tendency was for peripheral areas to be most affected by falling demand, and trend surfaces for individual industries would tend to exhibit a similar pattern. Thirdly, in the case of Basildon, and to a far lesser degree in Harlow, the residuals appear to be associated with extreme rates of growth, suggesting that growth has a quadratic effect. That is, areas of very fast expansion, with a high proportion of their employment in construction are as vulnerable to cyclical contractions and delays in investment as are areas of slow growth or absolute decline, where a similar cause might lead to the closure of existing, marginally profitable, businesses. In addition, the overall amplitude of the former group is enlarged because of its equally large downswing in unemployment.

Business Cycle Regions, 1951-1968. Previous sections of this chapter have been concerned with individual components of cyclical unemployment, without any objective attempt to recognise regional similarities in behaviour. Although many of the maps indicate such groupings it is valuable to probe more deeply by investigating the degree of similarity and the particular constituents of a discrete set of subregions.

Time-series inter-correlations are again used, allowing coefficients to be derived which indicate the degree of likeness between any pair of areas from an $n \times n$ matrix. An hypothetical set of series and their inter-correlations is described in Figure 3.8 to clarify the interpretation of coefficients. Thus low coefficients may be the result of changes in the absolute differences of amplitudes in two areas, to differences in trends, or to the presence of lags. The cofficients can then be used to derive a dendrogram with each linkage in the hierarchy drawn at the value to the coefficient between a pair of areas, or at the minimum value when one area is joined with several others.[7] In East Anglia the resulting sets based on the 1951-1968 series, shown in Figure 3.9, had a marked clustering, with a number of groups containing very high coefficients; each group was linked with others at relatively low levels. This condition implies low within—group variance in cyclical behaviour, but high between—group variance, a condition necessary for significant regionalization.

When mapped (Figure 3.10) moreover, these groups tend to have a high degree of internal contiguity, despite the lack of any such constraint in the analysis. Furthermore, the strongest linkages (correlations exceeding 0.9) emphasise the tendency for near neighbours to show similar responses. At the level at which the combination of groups leads to the sharpest decline in within-group variance there were four major clusters and two minor ones.

The largest and most diffuse was a "Mid-Anglian" sub-region which contained three main centres, Norwich, Ipswich and Colchester, all of which were relatively highly diversified and tended to conform fairly well with the regional series and with each other. Several of the less industrialized areas of the group were contiguous with these and appear to have had their courses largely determined by them. Linked with this group at a relatively low level was a small cluster consisting of Haverhill, Newmarket and Sudbury, themselves contiguous and abutting onto several members of the major group. All three were influenced, though in varying degrees, by town expansion schemes.

The second major group can be designated as the "Waveney Valley" sub-region, and consisted of two pairs of areas (Diss and Harleston, and Beccles and Bungay) each of which had very similar industrial compositions. Their forming of a tight-knit cluster, however, was apparently influenced most strongly by their contiguity.

This was less true of the third main group, however, which contained the whole of north Norfolk, and one anomalous area, Chelmsford, which was linked with the others at a very low level solely on the grounds of a similar upward trend though in every other respect it would normally have joined a different group. The distinguishing feature of the main portion of this cluster, however, was its relatively homogeneous industrial composition and low population density, ensuring that all its separate areas (except King's Lynn) suffered from the same trends both in general economic development and cyclical behaviour.

The fourth major cluster was also distinctive, having the most varied set of industrial bases, but forming a fairly compact cluster in south Essex and the coastal areas of Clacton, Harwich and Felixstowe.

Finally, a minor group is formed of the three areas which shared the blggest improvements in trend, Basildon, Great Yarmouth and Lowestoft, although in the last two, similarity of industrial structure was also a significant factor.

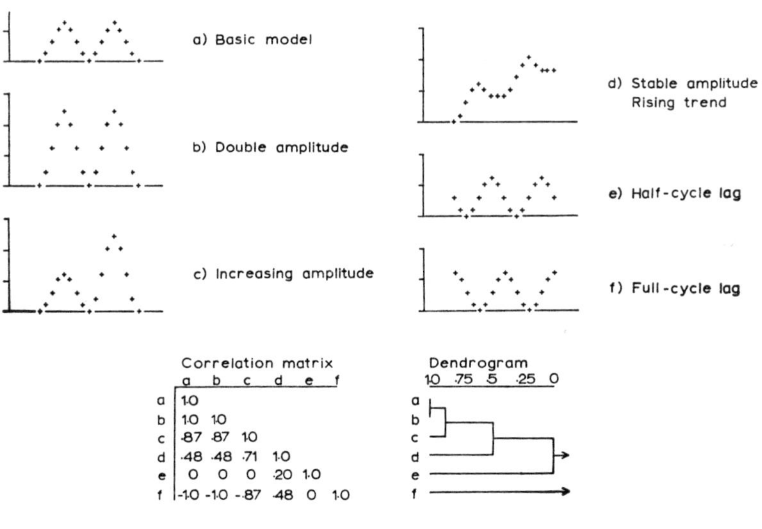

	a	b	c	d	e	f
a	1·0					
b	1·0	1·0				
c	·87	·87	1·0			
d	·48	·48	·71	1·0		
e	0	0	0	·20	1·0	
f	-1·0	-1·0	-·87	·48	0	1·0

Figure 3.8. Clustering in hypothetical time-series

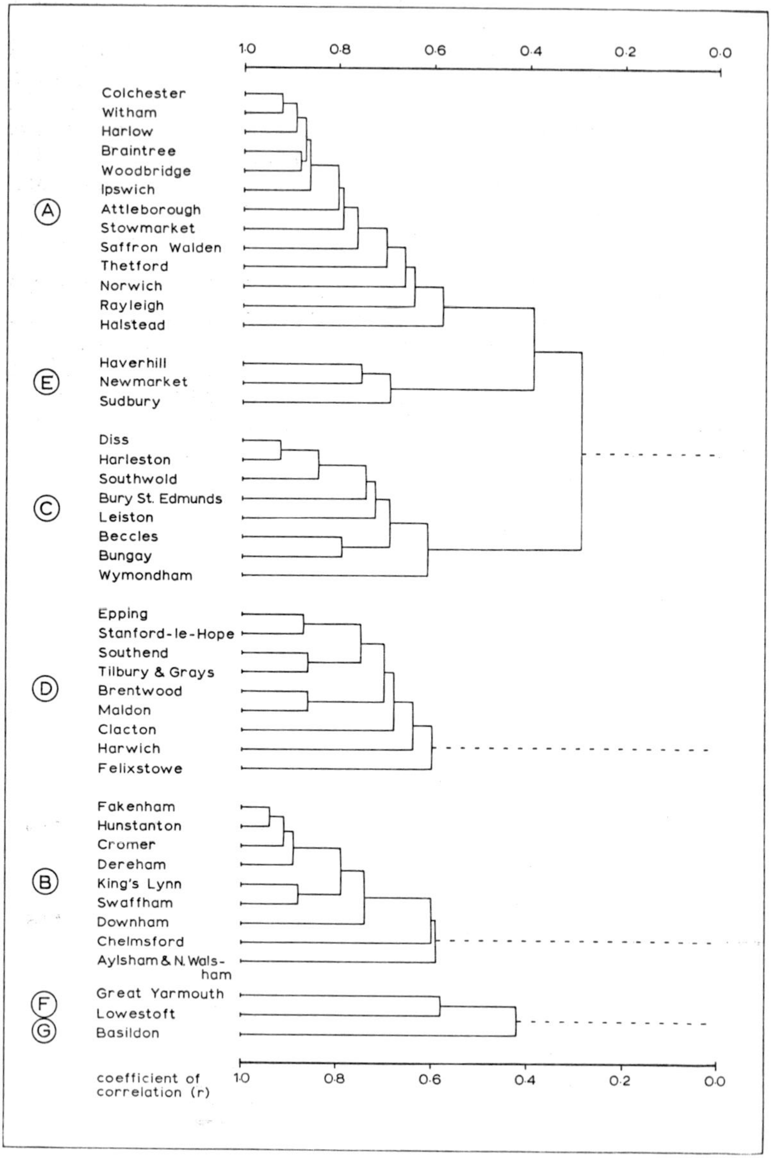

Figure 3·9. Dendrogram of time series inter-correlations, by exchange areas.

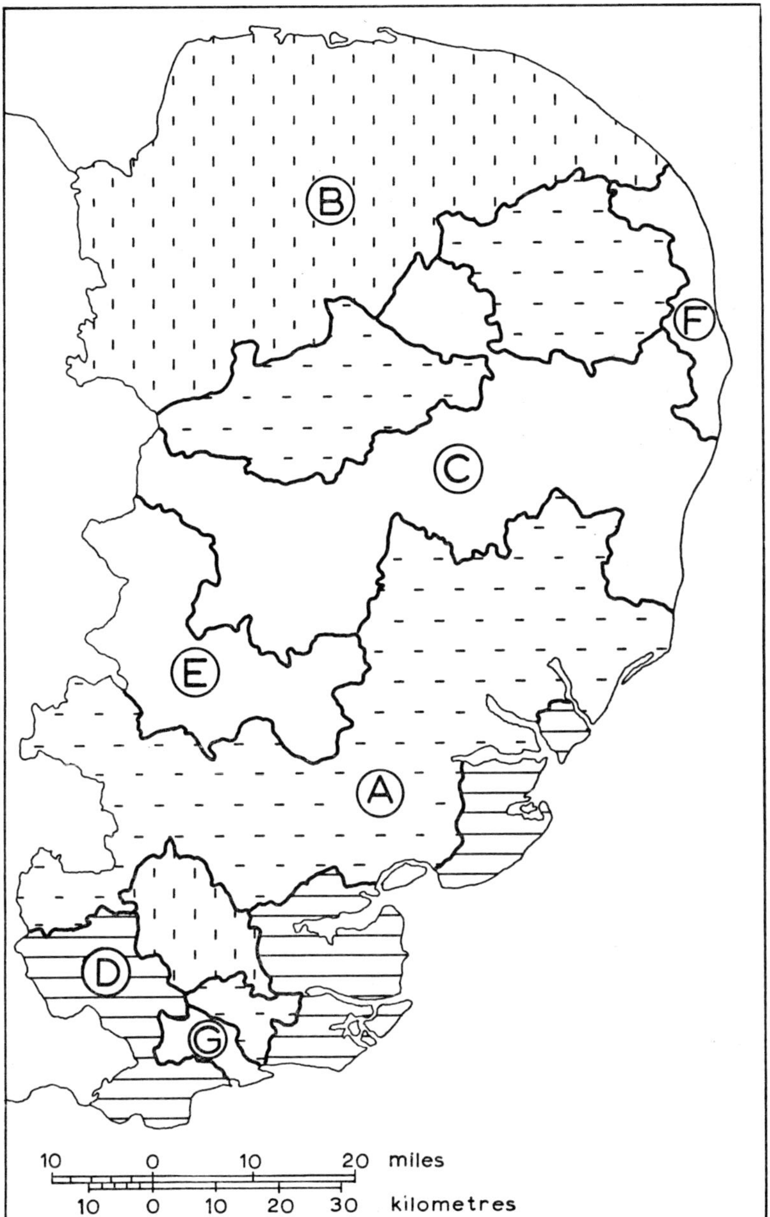

Figure 3.10. Business cycle regions in East Anglia

References

1. Haggett, P. (1971) Leads and lags in inter-regional systems: a study of the cyclic fluctuations in the South West economy; in *Spatial Policy Problems of the British Economy*, edited by Chisholm, M. & G. Manners, London.
2. Ya-lun Chou (1963) *Applied Business and Economic Statistics*, New York. pp. 471-560.
   Felner, W. (1956) *Trends and Cycles in Economic Activity*. New York.
   Marris, R. (1965) *Economic Arithmetic*. London.
3. Ministry of Labour (1965) Seasonal variations in unemployment. *Ministry of Labour Gazette*, 73, 382-6.
4. Moore, G. H. & J. Shiskin (1967) *Indicators of Business Expansions and Contractions N.B.E.R.* New York.
5. Vining, R. (1949) The regions as an economic entity and certain variations to be observed in the study of systems of regions. *American Economic Review*, 39, 100.
6. King, L. J., E. Casetti & D. Jeffrey (1969) Economic impulses in a regional system of cities: a study of spatial interaction. *Regional Studies*, 3, 213-18.
7. Sokal, R. R. & P. H. Sneath (1963) *Principles of Numerical Taxonomy*. San Francisco.

IV

Amplitude and Timing: a Multivariate Analysis

In this chapter the purpose is to decompose the three cycles completed since 1951 into their separate phases and to test the validity of the patterns of responses hypothesised in Chapter 2.

Cycle Amplitudes: 1951-66

Each of the six phases described in Figures 4.1 to 4.3 differed, even if only marginally, from the others. Only the upswing and subsequent downswing between 1955 and 1961 were closely similar, in the distribution of their amplitudes; the correlation coefficient (r) between the two patterns was 0·94. In contrast there was practically no correlation ($r=0{\cdot}18$) between that downswing and the upswing occurring between 1961 and 1963. The phases also differed in their severity, with the second cycle (1955-61) having markedly the greater amplitudes. During this cycle almost half of the areas had amplitudes of more than 2·5%, whereas in the first cycle (1951-55), half of the amplitudes fell below 1·0%. The third cycle (1961-66) suffered amplitudes which were about mid-way between the other two. Thus, although the general distribution of amplitudes did not change radically, it is clear that cycles were not stable oscillations. Hence it can be expected that the variables in the hypothesis differed in their importance from one phase to the next, as is evident in Table 4.1. Of the spatial structure variables only the national and regional indices were consistently significant, while rurality proved to be marginally important by itself only in the second cycle. Industrial composition likewise fulfilled its expected role in each phase but employment change, while giving a significantly better explanation when expressed as a quadratic, was important only in the first cycle and the last upswing.

Table 4.1 also shows that no single variable accounted for more than a small proportion (about 30%) of the variation in any phase. However, since there is no major problem of multicollinearity among these variables it is expected that considerably greater explanations can be obtained in multiple regression models. Moreover, as indicated in Table 4.2, which summarizes the results from this analysis, not only can about half the variance in amplitudes be explained, but also it is necessary to use all three factors (spatial structure, industrial composition and employment

Table 4.1 Correlation coefficients (r) between amplitude and independent variables; by cycle phase, 1951-66.

	Phase					
	First cycle		Second cycle		Third cycle	
	Up	Down	Up	Down	Up	Down
National index of location	–·50	–·44	–·57	–·51	–·34	–·56
Regional index of location	–·38	–·33	–·42	–·38	–·61	–·32
Local population field	–·16	–·01	–·30	–·33	–·24	–·04
Central plane rank	–·32	–·00	–·32	–·32	–·24	–·04
Employment change	·32	·54	·16	·10	·46	·15
Industrial structure (% in vulnerable base)	·53	·35	·42	·47	·34	·26

Significance levels with 43 degrees of freedom 95%: r=+/– 0·25
99%: r=+/– 0·34

change) to do so. This, in a phenomenon subject to large random and differential trend elements is a satisfactory, if by no means complete, explanation which would be difficult to improve without incorporating dummy variables to account for the random movements.

Although the same variables were usually involved at each phase their importance, estimated from their significance levels (students "t") and standardized regression coefficients,[1] varied considerably between cycles. Industrial composition weakened relative to the other sets, suggesting that amplitudes were increasingly influenced by rates of investment and growth in employment and also with location in relation to other parts of the region and other regions in Britain. This occurred despite the lack of any marked tendency for areas to become more alike either in their overall composition or in the proportion of their employment in unstable basic industries. By contrast, spatial structure became stronger at the two upper scales (national and regional) reflecting expansion in inter-regional and intra-regional flows, making marginal areas increasingly vulnerable to shifts in demand. Thirdly, the role of employment changes also varied. Although when viewed as a single variable these always improved with a quadratic function this was no longer true when incorporated in a multivariate analysis, applying only in the first and third cycles both of which coincided more closely with periods of sharply increased investment in a number of localized developments.

The first upswing was a relatively mild movement following the 1951 balance of payments crisis caused by an increase in import prices, occurring at a time when demand in all sectors of the British economy was at a high level.[2] In rural areas agriculture was still operating at a low level of mechanisation, giving it a high (relative to later cycles) demand for labour and this, combined with increasing demand for labour at military bases gave most of them quite small amplitudes. The highest amplitudes were in fact experienced in resorts and a few manufacturing areas with unstable bases, with agricultural areas forming a second tier. At the other extreme were areas, clustered in southern Essex, most of which were dominated by growth industries and located close to the main national markets. Thus in the first upswing the principal factor conbuting to the distribution was industrial composition, giving rise to a

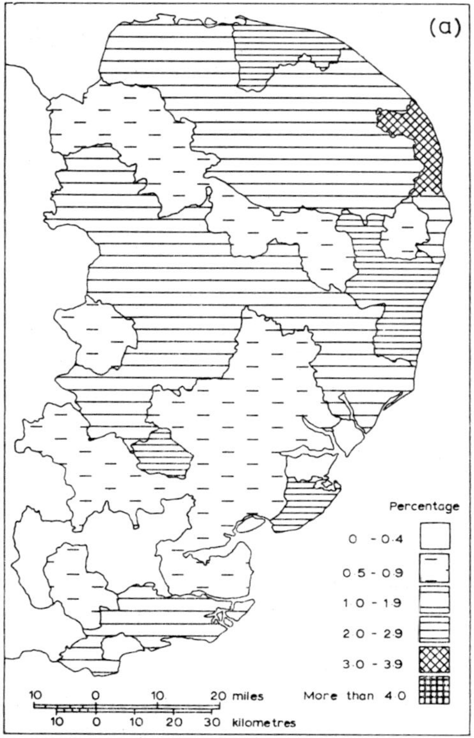

Figure 4.1 Cycle amplitudes 1951-1955

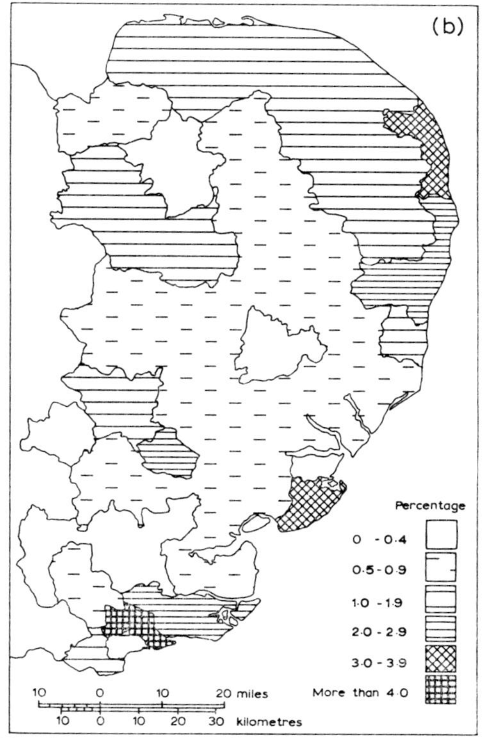

Figure 4.1 (*a*) Upswing Figure 4.1 (*b*) Downswing

Table 4.2 Abstract of best regressions between amplitudes and independent variables

First Upswing	First Downswing
Industrial composition (+)	National index of location (–)
National index of location (–)	Industrial composition (+)
Employment change (–)	Employment change (–)
Local population potential (+)	Local population potential (+)
Regional index of location (–)	
$r^2=0{\cdot}58$	$r^2=0{\cdot}48$
Second Upswing	*Second Downswing*
National index of location (–)	National index of location (–)
Industrial composition (+)	Industrial composition (+)
Regional index of location (–)	Employment change (+)
Employment change (+)	
$r^2=0{\cdot}55$	$r^2=0{\cdot}48$
Third Upswing	*Third Downswing*
Regional index of location (–)	National index of location (–)
Employment change (–)	Employment change (–)
National index of location (–)	Industrial composition (+)
Industrial composition (+)	
$r^2=0{\cdot}51$	$r^2=0{\cdot}56$

spatial pattern more variegated than in other phases. However, this factor accounted for no more than 27% of the variance, leaving significant residuals which were best explained by the national index and the rate of employment change in each area. To experience low amplitudes, areas had to "score" well on at least any two of the above three variables: the better the balance, the lower the amplitude. When these and two other less significant variables (local population potential and the regional index) are included 58% of the variance can be explained, and the number of large residuals is reduced to a handful. In most cases these can be attributed to local factors, where areas were dominated by single large firms with non-conforming responses; Halstead and Leiston had much greater amplitudes than expected, Beccles and Witham had smaller ones.

The subsequent downswing was not an exact image of the upswing even though the two phases were quite closely matched. Most areas underwent some sort of trend, making the two movements unequal, with the majority having slightly smaller downswings. The result was an adjustment in the redistribution of amplitudes, particularly among some of the former positive residuals, making their responses more like those of their neighbours and causing industrial composition to become displaced as the leading independent variable by the national index of location. Again the location of major residuals pointed to localised factors operating in highly specialised areas. Most of the larger, diversified centres were closely predicted by the combination of factors.

In the second cycle (1955-61) the phases were marked in all areas by a larger upswing than at any other time, followed, in a number (especially in North Norfolk) by a strong upward trend in unemployment which weakened the force of their downswings. As a result the two phases

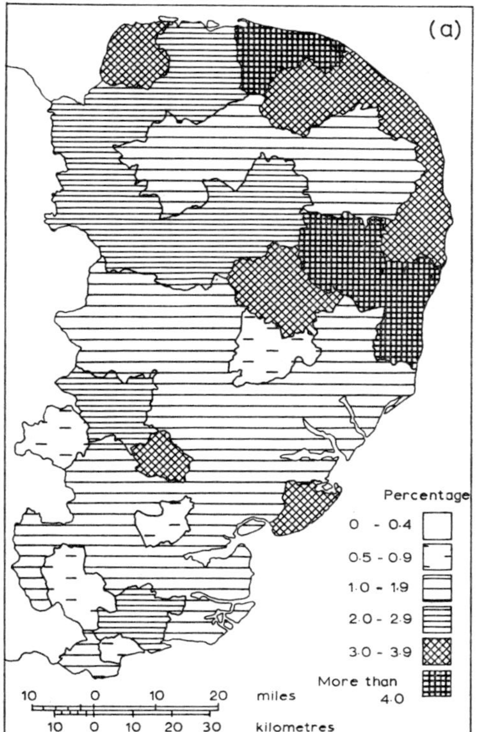

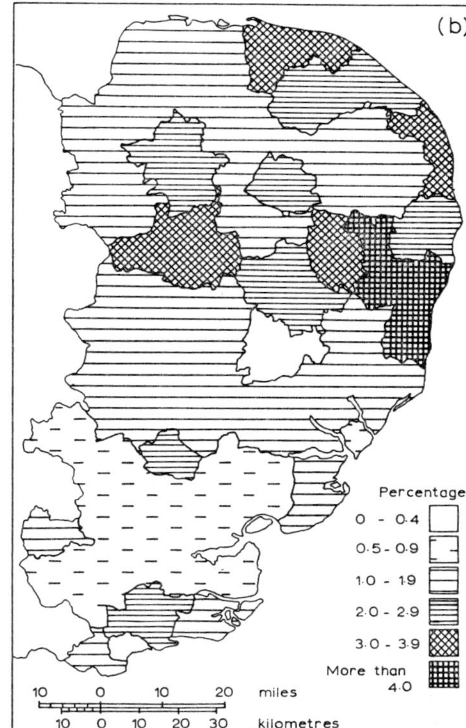

Figure 4·2 Cycle amplitudes, 1955-1961

Figure 4.2 (*a*) Upswing Figure 4.2 (*b*) Downswing

consisted of different distributions which, while retaining the basic north-south dichotomy, were associated with differences in the parameters of their regression equations. In the upswing the greatest amplitudes (in some cases over 6%) were experienced in northeast Suffolk, followed by areas which usually combined agricultural and resort functions which, in turn, were more vulnerable than areas with agricultural bases alone. Industrial composition, however, only accounted for extremes, and was markedly less important than the national index of location in explaining the overall pattern. Moreover, these factors were strongly reinforced by regional indices and employment changes, so that in total about 55% of the variance was explained.

The duration of the downswing, approximately from 1958 to 1961, covered the period during which DATAC status was conferred on north Norfolk and northeast Suffolk which returned to fairly low levels of unemployment (in some cases this was lower than at previous comparable phases) while most of rural Norfolk had only minor improvements before the third upswing began. As a result the level of explained variace fell to below 50% and there was a readjustment of factors in the regression equation, with the regional index becoming insignificant, and industrial composition becoming more important.

Entering the third cycle, amplitudes exhibited a continuation of the trends noted in the previous phase. Against this background the set of responses generally resembled those of the second cycle, with higher amplitudes in the upswing than in the downswing, especially among areas suffering most from worsening trends. In the upswing this brought about a distinct intra-regional variation with areas least favoured on the regional index of location having the highest amplitudes, made worse by contraction or very slow rates of growth in long term demand for labour. The resulting pattern exhibited a clustering in north Norfolk, with the exception of King's Lynn where growth rates were much higher following early industrial growth in association with its town development scheme. A much smaller group with high amplitudes still existed in northeast Suffolk, but most of these areas had generated sufficient new industry to suppress the upswing well below previous levels. At the other extreme, areas in west Suffolk with town development schemes, and Great Yarmouth and Lowestoft had trends in the opposite direction, giving them much smaller amplitudes than previously. Within the southern half of the region the effect was more closely related to the national index of location, producing a division between east and west not explained by either of the two main factors.

Finally, in the downswing there was a repetition of the dominance of the national index of location as areas with most potential for absorbing unemployed resources were located mainly around the eastern side of the region. In the remainder of East Anglia areas in the southwestern quarter, including expansion schemes, had little such capacity; in the north capacity existed but opportunities for growth were lacking (except in King's Lynn).

Reviewing these phases as a continuous sequence of oscillations it is possible to seek common paths through which patterns of amplitudes were determined. Above all, it becomes clear that sub-regional analysis

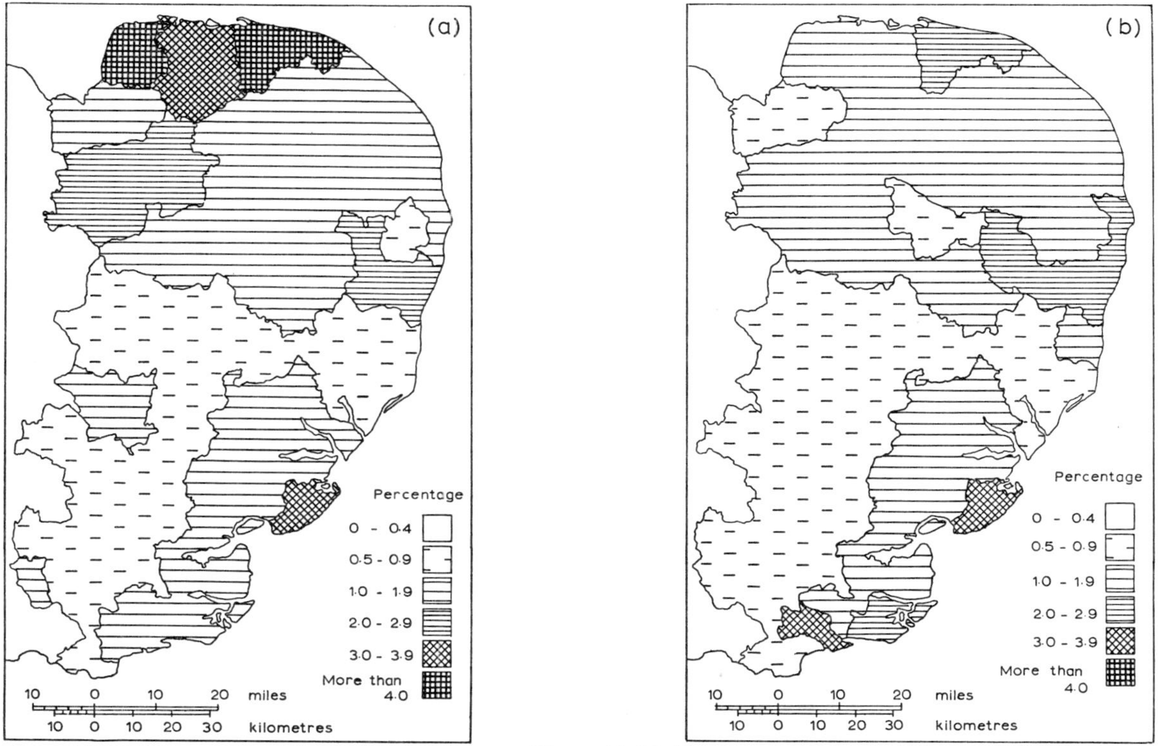

Figure 4.3 Cycle amplitudes, 1961-1966

Figure 4.3 (*a*) Upswing

Figure 4.3 (*b*) Downswing

provides strong evidence of the role of intra-industrial variations. In particular, spatial structure is seen to be more significant than either of the other two sets of variables and provided the main channel along which cyclical changes had their differing impact in every phase but one. That occasion was dominated by industrial composition but although this factor was significant in all phases its importance appeared to diminish, regardless of the severity of the cycle. This does not imply that industrial composition might not be dominant in cycles of the greatest severity but there is no evidence here that it would. On the other hand, the role of changes in employment appears to be subject to the nature of the cycle, such that rapid growth acts as an insurance against the more severe swings, although the effect in these series tended to be only marginal. In fact, the significance of high rates of investment and employment growth is best seen in the minor recession in 1956, when areas responding most were characterized by these features; the effect can be seen by comparing the areas in Group D in Figure 3.3 with other groups whose growth potential was much less but whose overall amplitudes were far greater.

Finally, the patterns of residuals from the regression analysis suggest that these three basic sets of variables, while accounting for little more than a half of the variance, cannot profitably be augmented by others except on a piecemeal basis. The largest residuals were found among small, specialized areas, whose major firms behave individualistically and, in a statistical sense, unpredictably. Without knowing more about the health of their past balance sheets and employment policies it is impossible to justify the inclusion of a variable to represent their presence. This is not to imply that nonconforming behaviour did not also occur among firms in larger areas, but the greater population of firms there ensured greater predictability of aggregate conditions. The only major industrial area with an average residual greater than 0·5 S.E. was Southend, though the neighbouring area of Rayleigh averaged 1·0 S.E.; in both actual amplitudes exceeded predicted. Here, the difference was due largely to weak industrial classification; though both had important engineering and electrical sectors these tended to contain firms in the competitive consumer goods side of the industry which was generally more volatile. On the other hand there was a high degree of accuracy in the prediction of the areas lying at the extremes on each of the variables and this, together with relatively small standard errors, makes it possible to have confidence that prediction of future patterns, if not of actual rates, can be approached with fair moderate accuracy.

Cycle Turning Points: 1951-1966

Like amplitudes there was no complete consistency between timing at the four cyclical turning points: patterns varied between adjacent points and from cycle to cycle. Nevertheless, the aggregative patterns discussed in the previous chapter provided at least some support for believing that variations had a basis in the character of the regional economy. Although basically the same set of variables is used their relationship with timing tended to be very much weaker than with amplitudes. In addition there was greater dependence on the nature of the turning point; for example the period from 1955 to 1957 included a series of crises,[3] giving rise to a minor recession in unemployment, upsetting the patterns of turning points through most of the second cycle, and the start of the upswing in 1966 was dominated by deflationary measures making most areas respond in concert. In both cases correlations with all parameters were very low.

The degree of variegation in patterns of timing noted in the previous chapter made it inevitable that correlations with the elements of spatial structure should be low. Of the four variables none were significantly associated at even half of the turns and only three of a possible 48 coefficients lay above the 99% confidence level. Coefficients above the 95% confidence level, moreover, were mainly clustered in the national and regional indices, usually with a negative sign, indicating a lag in peripheral areas. But the relationships were so weak that they cannot be taken as evidence of spatial movements across the region.

Similarly weak correlations with changes in employment also occurred, although, as with amplitudes, a slight improvement was brought about by using a quadratic function; however, within the range of values experienced in different areas this only implied a diminishing marginal effect of higher rates of growth. In general rapid growth tended to make areas lead at the beneficial turns, though the evidence at the start of upswings was weaker.

In theory a significant association ought to be found between timing and industrial composition due to differential changes in the demand for goods and services. However, the available data do not facilitate a division of industries by probable characteristics in timing and the unemployment series of S.I.C. Orders exhibit no marked inter-industrial differences. The 'next-best" approach is to employ the unstable basic sector (as defined above) since leads and lags can be viewed as the product of larger or smaller responses at each step in each cyclical phase. However, in spite of this device correlations between timing and industrial composition were very low, and their signs contained inconsistencies. Large unstable sectors were linked with leads at the start of the upswing and lags at the end, as expected, but the other two turning points were indeterminate.

Finally, the patterns in Figure 3.5 suggested the need to include a variable accounting for the magnitude of the swing immediately preceding a turning point since, all other things being equal, the greater the rise or fall the later will be the turn. Thus a positive correlation between timing and previous amplitude existed at the end of each downswing and upswing. Although not strictly related to regional economic structure like the other variables, this is a factor which helps to explain occasional distributions which contain anomalies.

The relatively low and unstable correlations between timing and the independent variables are predictable when account is taken of the tenuous basis for expecting such associations, since it has been argued that the transmission process, which provides a theoretical mechanism, is likely to exist in a form too complex to provide well defined patterns. Further difficulties arise when this is related to the differing contexts within which a series of turning points occur. These, the changing character of the regional economy and variations in the nature of cycles, make timing much less easy to forecast than amplitudes, even when a multivariate analysis is employed. What tended to occur was a large range in the proportion of variance explained, with some turning points exhibiting almost random patterns while others strongly reflected regional parameters, in contrast with amplitudes where the proportion remained almost constant. In timing, the highest coefficient of multiple correlation (r^2) reached ·55 but most, though statistically significant, fell between ·25 and ·40. In addition, there was greater variability in the significance of individual factors; on no ocasasions were the components of the best regressions for comparable turning points alike. Nevertheless, the results prove to be encouraging and suggest that, even if an explanation of the transmission process is lacking, the timing of responses does tend to be determined in large measure by the nature of the regional economy.

Because each turning point is treated separately it is valuable to present each as a single distribution. This is done in Figure 4.4 which begins with the end of the first upswing (median date, second half of 1952) and finishes with the end of the third downswing (second half 1964): the start of the fourth upswing, which is included in the analysis, is not mapped since no areas fell into a definable lagging group. In order to simplify the maps only those areas which lagged (that is, by being behind the median group in the frequency distributions of Table 3.2), are shaded and no account is taken of the amount of lead or lag in the maps, although specific values are used in the analysis. These relate to the position of the half-year in which each area's turning points occurred in relation to the entire series. Thus July/51/January 1952 is accorded the value 1·0, January/July 52 is 2·0 . . . to January/July 66 which has the value 32·0. A synopsis of results describing the best correlates at each turning point is presented in Table 4.3.

The early 1950's which began with an upswing in unemployment was also a period of rapid growth in employment in East Anglia and in demand for consumer durables and investment goods throughout Britain. Not surprisingly, therefore, the main factor determining when areas stopped their cyclical upswings was their current industrial expansion, giving an imperfect north-south division between lagging and leading areas. Where residuals occurred the factor best offsetting them was found to be location within the region. Thus, for example, if two areas had equal rates of change in employment the one with the highest regional index of location would normally have been the first to respond to the restoration of demand.

A similar pattern was carried through the ensuing downswing with rural areas covering most of Norfolk and east Suffolk tending to lag at the start. A cluster in Essex which also lagged contained a number of areas for which this classification is only partly valid since their unemployment throughout the cycle had altered very little between trough and peak. Even so, the distribution conformed quite well to elements in the regional economy, with all the high ranking centres leading and slow-growing, rural areas with large unstable components lagging.

There then followed, through the mid-1950's, a period of very mixed responses. The end of the downswing was led by areas with no common characteristics and lagging areas, with the exception of a cluster with peripheral locations and weak growth trends in East Suffolk, were dispersed. The distribution at the start of the following upswing was more

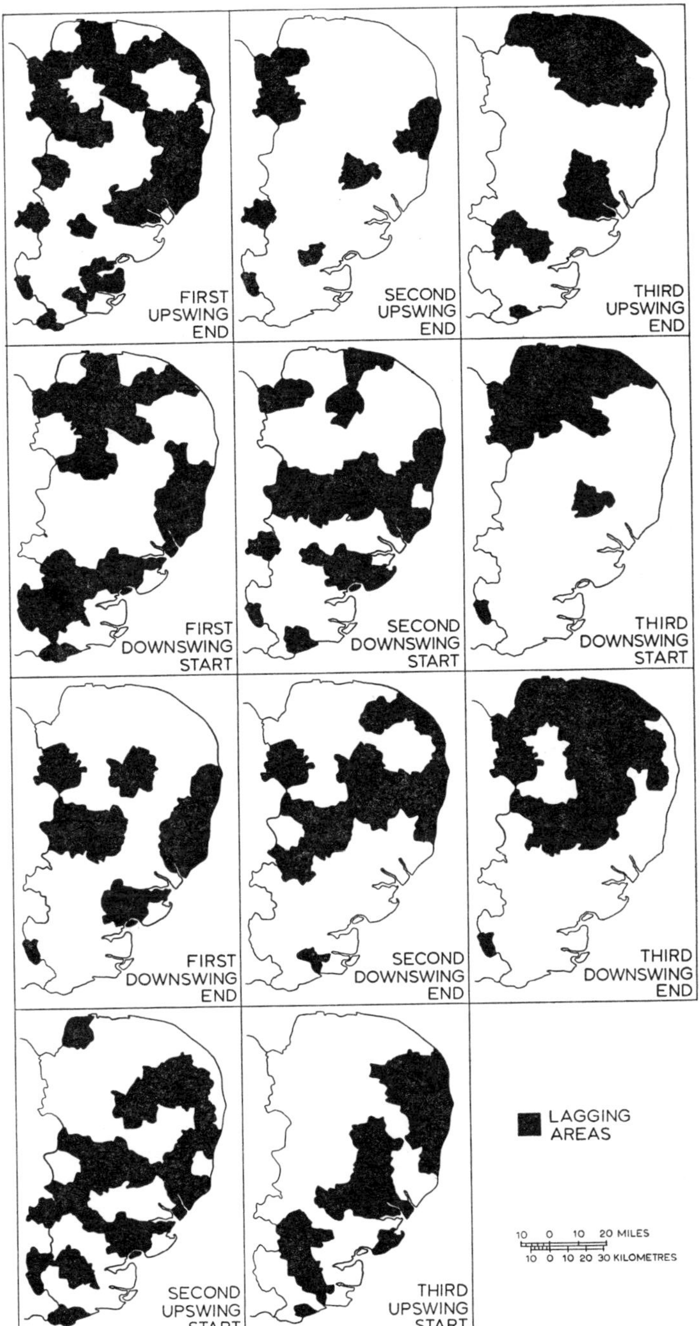

Figure 4.4 The timing of cyclical turning points, 1951-1966

closely related to industrial composition, however, with areas dominated by unstable bases tending to lead, giving rise to a highly variegated pattern. Even so, the correlation was prevented from rising to a satisfactory level by the impact of the minor recession of 1956, which caused several industrial areas in Essex, with only moderately unstable industrial bases to join a group in north Norfolk (whose presence was expected) in leading the upswing.

The second cycle was the most severe of the three but while turning points were still widely spread in time their geographical distribution was poorly related to regional parameters. This appears to run counter to expectation since areas with higher amplitudes normally take longer to reach a turning point, other things being equal. However, this was a period of some readjustment in the region, with government support given to two sets of development areas (in north Norfolk and northeast Suffolk). These two groups responded quite differently under this influence, and within the latter group there were different timings with Harleston and Bungay leading while Diss and Southwold both lagged.

From then until the end of the third cycle turning points were continuously related significantly with the structure of the regional economy.

Table 4.3 Abstract of best regressions between timing and independent variables

Upswing	*Downswing*
First Cycle	
– end Employment change (–) Regional index of location (–) Previous amplitude (+) $r^2=0{\cdot}30$	
	– start Central place rank (+) Industrial composition (–) Previous amplitude (–) Employment change (–) $r^2=0{\cdot}40$
	– end National index of location (–) $r^2=0{\cdot}05$
Second Cycle	
– start Industrial composition (–) $r^2=0{\cdot}14$	
– end National index of location (–) Employment change (+) $r^2=0{\cdot}12$	
	– start National index of location (–) $r^2=0{\cdot}07$

Table 4.3—continued

	– end Previous amplitude (+) Local population potential (+) Employment change (–) $r^2=0{\cdot}45$
Third Cycle	
– start National index of location (–) National index of location (+) $r^2=0{\cdot}34$	
– end Regional index of location (–) Employment change (–) $r^2=0{\cdot}28$	
	– start Regional index of location (–) Employment change (–) National index of location (+) $r^2=0{\cdot}55$
	– end Employment change (–) National index of location (–) Industrial composition (+) $r^2=0{\cdot}33$
Fourth Cycle	
– start Local population potential (+) $r^2=0{\cdot}07$	

The speed of the return to low levels of unemployment around 1960 depended chiefly upon the amplitude of the downswing, but once account has been taken of this there were also significant correlations with local population potential and growth potential. Low densities of employment opportunities, related to the first of these, influenced the rate of absorption of men out of work, as expected. This was reinforced where growth was slow, and this combination of factors was most effective in northeast Norfolk plus several other rural areas. At the other extreme the main group of leaders was found in Essex where opposite conditions existed. Residuals from these groups occurred in north Norfolk, where the downswing was terminated early by the onset of a marked upward trend in unemployment, and Great Yarmouth and Haverhill where recent accelerations in growth caused them to continue improving and, hence, to lag.

Most areas then had a period of stable, low rates before starting the third upswing in 1961. In this time the process of readjustment continued to bring about a region with more clear-cut geographical distinctions. The two New Towns had become well established and, although still exhibiting the fastest growth rates in the region, had more normal industrial compositions. Secondly, town expansion schemes were being added to the region, mainly in west Suffolk, and beginning to have an impact on the pattern of responses. Third, the brief period of DATAC status in northeast Suffolk had had some influence on stability following the creation of new jobs, but the same status had no significant effect in north Norfolk, which experienced markedly worsening trends, especially in the early 1960's. Together these factors brought about a set of responses which were different from preceding cycles and also more closely aligned with elements of the regional economy.

Thus the distribution at the start of the third upswing was largely expected, with the main leading group found in a contiguous cluster of rural areas. Additional leaders in the southern half of the region consisted mostly of areas whose high rates of industrial expansion made them vulnerable to a sharp increase in interest rates following the rise in Bank Rate in 1961 from 5% to 7%. In such conditions the effect on industrial expansion and relocation can take the form of large delays in completion since the cost to most firms is substantially increased. Although the general pattern was expected the composition of the best regression took no account of differences in growth rates. Instead, an anomalous negative association with the national index occurred, but this cannot be interpreted as being in any way significant. On the other hand, when this variable is suppressed there was a significant relationship with the regional index; areas with high values usually lagged, conforming with the hypothetical condition in which the better located among competing areas are less vulnerable.

Once under way the upswing continued in most areas for approximately two years, terminating in 1963 when it was quickly followed by the start of the downswing. Thus the distributions at both of these turning points were similar, though the latter, needing extra impetus, was more distinctly segregated. In both the basic relationships were negative correlations between timing and regional indices and employment changes. Compared with equivalent turning points in previous cycles the result was a marked clustering in north and central Norfolk, particularly in the downswing, confirming the economic weaknesses of these areas. At the other extreme the main leaders were areas with strong growth potential, now released by falling interest rates, and rising consumer demand.

In the subsequent downswing unemployment rates fell sharply, in many areas to levels at which spare manpower was almost completely absorbed. In these areas, located mainly in fast growing zones with high national indices, the return to low rates was carried out very early (in some cases in 1964). As a result the progression of turning points contained a distinct pattern, broken only where expansion schemes (planned or unplanned) penetrated the northern half of the region. These included the developing town of Thetford, the two bases of gas exploration at Great Yarmouth and Lowestoft, and Leiston where the construction of the nuclear power station created a large local demand for labour. In the remaining areas of the north the downswing proceeded slowly, and in many cases was terminated only by the start of the final upswing in 1965/66.

At that point, however, they proved to be the leaders, making their turns before the mass of areas whose timing awaited the battery of deflationary measures taken between late 1965 and mid-1966. The lack of any distinct lags, with two-thirds of the areas turning together, accounted for the poor correlation at this point, though it is likely that had there been fewer direct interventions to lower the level of demand the distribution of turning points would have closely reflected location and employment changes since the labour market in many areas, especially in Essex, had become very tight. Under such conditions employers are likely to hold labour for as long as possible in the expectation that they would have to compete for it in the downswing. Selective Employment Tax, announced in May (and implemented in September) 1966 reduced this tendency, however, by making it more expensive to "hoard" labour, especially in service industries.

It is impossible to carry the analysis of timing any further in the series since, although many areas appeared to enter a downswing in 1967, there is no evidence from the basic set of data that this was a true end to their upswings. In other cases the upswing continued unabated into 1968 and beyond, making a frequency distribution of timing unfeasible.

Additional Questions

(i) Failure to explain more than about half the variance in amplitudes raises the question whether this is attributable to the mildness of cycles between 1951 and 1966. Unfortunately, amplitudes were too alike to investigate this. However, an analysis of unadjusted three monthly changes in unemployment through the period 1964 to 1966 suggested that there is some validity in this notion. The range of amplitudes experienced in the eleven quarters of this period in the regional series was from 0·04 per cent to 1·28 per cent, and the mean deviation of the 45 areas from the regional values lay between 0·35 per cent and 1·00 per cent.

Now, to test whether the relationship exists, a rank correlation can be carried out between the amplitude (or mean deviation) for the eleven quarters and the coefficients (r^2) found between amplitude and the independent variables. The most important finding from this analysis is a very close correlation between the effect of inter-industrial variations and the severity of changes. The rank correlations with amplitudes and mean deviation were both above 0·8. Of the remaining variables the locational indices at national and regional scales also tended to become more important as amplitudes rose, but the effect on the remainder was negligible. However, since the three major variables in the multiple regression analyses were involved, it followed that the overall explanation of amplitudes was improved during more severe changes.

(ii) While it is accepted that all industries do not behave homogeneously it is also possible to indicate the degree to which industries deviate from this ideal. Analogous with the analysis of conformity among areas, the series for each industry (S.I.C. Orders) is correlated with the regional series. Also, by experimenting with current and lagged correlations it is possible to identify the role of industrial responses.

A critical difference is found between the manufacturing and service sectors. While five out of seven industries in the latter group had correlations significant at over the 90% level with the regional series only five out of fourteen of the former group did so. Construction, which has many of the attributes of the tertiary sector, was also significantly associated. Equally important, only one of those service industries was not best correlated in a lagged form. That is, the service industries, and construction, as expected from their marked orientation, responded to changes in manufacturing.

(iii) The time series of areas were adjusted for seasonal fluctuations but not for trend since it was argued that the latter could not be adequately distinguished. However, a question is raised whether there might be an association between changes in the strength of local economies and changes in their amplitudes between one cycle and the next. To investigate the relationship changes of ranks in employment growth and the amplitude during upswings are compared. Where opposite signs occurred there is evidence that accelerated growth (either absolute, or relative to other areas) was associated with diminishing amplitudes, and *vice versa*. In East Anglia, opposite signs tended to occur twice as frequently as like signs.

References

1. King, L. J. (1969). *Statistical Analysis in Geography*. New Jersey. p. 140.

2. Worswick, G. D. N. (1962) The British economy, 1950-1959 in Worswick and P. Ady *The British Economy in the Nineteen-fifties*. Oxford pp. 1-27.

3. Scott, M. F. G. (1962) The balance of payments crises, in Worswick and Ady op cit. p. 218-23.

V

Summary and Conclusion

At the outset of this study the general statement was made that cyclical responses are expected to be strongly related to geographical factors. Much evidence had already been collected about regional cycles, but it was believed that the scale of analysis should be shifted to concentrate upon small areas because regional studies cannot encompass the range of variables considered important in determining the distribution of responses. This shift in scale necessitated two decisions of fundamental importance; namely, in which region to base the study, and with what data to carry out the analysis. For the first, it was argued that East Anglia supplied the regional requirements; for the second, the most valuable source of data are monthly unemployment statistics, whose areal and temporal coverage outweighed their minor inaccuracies. On this basis the general hypothesis stated above is found to be significantly valid, although in detail there were important differences in the strengths of the various elements in the economic landscape.

Summary of Findings

The principal conclusions reached in this study relate to the impact of cyclical fluctuations upon the rates of unemployment in employment exchange areas and can be summarized according to the distributions associated with each cyclical parameter.

(a) Timing. Previous studies have, unintentionally, made it clear that it is necessary to distinguish four, rather than two, turning points in each cycle found in the seasonally adjusted series. Given these, differentiation in the timing of movements becomes more intelligible, in addition to the turning points having greater meaning.

(i) Variations in timing are clearest when, first, the turning point is a simple one (that is, associated with only one crisis, in the case of the upturn, rather than several in close succession, as through 1955-1957) and, second, when the gradual diffusion of cyclical effects is not overridden by sweeping governmental actions.

(ii) Correlations between timing and individual elements in the economic landscape tend to be weak. Satisfactory statistical explanations are achieved only when the variables are combined. Evidence from turning points in the period 1951-1966 indicates the best combination to have consisted of employment changes and spatial structure measured at the national and regional scales.

(iii) Where, as in the majority of cases, the distribution of turning points is significantly associated, areas tended to move in contiguous sub-regional *blocs,* with those areas which were economically most "healthy" lagging at the upturns and leading at all other times. Least "healthy" areas had the opposite features, except at the end of the downswing when their weak demand for labour tended to terminate the recovery in their unemployment series at an early stage.

(b) Amplitude. The impact of a cycle in each area was measured by calculating the difference between peak and trough unemployment rates in the multiplicatively adjusted series.

(i) Amplitude, like timing, had relatively weak correlations with individual variables, although it was found that inter-industrial and intra-industrial elements were both significant, the latter being dominated by spatial structure.

(ii) The role of employment changes is slightly more complex than other independent variables. Generally a quadratic function fitted the association better than a linear one, indicating that when areas have extreme growth rates (more than 10% per annum) they become as vulnerable as areas which are stagnant or declining. Over the range of growth rates contained in East Anglia, however, the quadratic function describes only a diminishing degree of stabilization resulting from each additional increment to the rate of growth.

(iii) An additional feature, related to economic trends, is the "retardation effect". Areas which fall in the growth rankings tend to occupy more vulnerable positions in the amplitude rankings.

(iv) While individual variables are capable of only weak explanations, at best, there tended to be enough complementarity between inter-industrial and intra-industrial elements to raise correlations considerably: the proportion of variance explained, (r^2) was increased from a maximum of about 0·3 for simple correlations to about 0·5, or more, for multiple correlations.

(v) The three completed cycles in this study all had similar amplitudes, but by analysis of seasonally unadjusted series from part of the most recent upswing (post 1966) it appears that a significant relationship exists between the magnitude of a cyclical phase and the strength of the inter-industrial control and, to a lesser extent, the regional and national spatial structures in determining the distribution of responses.

(c) Regions. The geographical expression of cyclical impacts is best summarized in a classification of areas according to the shape of their adjusted employment series. This usually showed areas to form contiguous *blocs* each of which was relatively homogeneous in terms of timing and amplitude in the upswing and downswing. Relating this to the hypotheses discussed in chapter 3, it is clear that the distribution of responses tended to be spatially, rather than hierarchically, controlled and that areal similarities were more important than areal linkages.

Further Questions

In this study the aim has been simply to describe and explain the distribution of cyclical parameters working from the hypothesis that they have geographical controls. In carrying this out the novel approach of investigating *micro*-regional variations was used, and the following outstanding questions can also be related to this scale of analysis.

First, it is most evident that more studies of the transmission process are necessary. Even though it has been argued that cycles tend to originate ubiquitously and that transmission tends to be anticipated this avoids the basic question of how areas are influenced by their linkages. To this end there would need to be vastly improved data, allowing rigorous input-output analysis based on sectoral and areal monetary flows. This is recognised as unlikely ever to be provided, but it means that with present knowledge it is impossible to do more than interpret circumstantial evidence.

Secondly, problems remain concerning the nature of intra-industrial variation. It has been demonstrated that these account for a large proportion of the variation in responses, but it is equally clear that each industry has its own pattern of internal variation. Even if this is partly explained by the aggregative nature of industrial classification it can be postulated that much of value stands to be gained from further researches of the same period and in the same regions.

Thirdly, this study of the distribution of responses has been only one aspect of several which might be undertaken. On the one hand, there is room for fruitful studies of the role of cycles in regional development, possibly (but not necessarily) including medium-term fluctuations in the list of factors relevant to the planning process. For example, there is evidence of cyclical variations in the volume of industrial movement which can be related to changes in industrial production and the availability of investment funds, as well as the level of regional incentives. Likewise, cyclical fluctuations may be reflected in substitutions, temporary or permanent, in the use of resources, including land. On the other hand, though probably less fruitful, there may be value in investigating the geographical contribution to the origin of cycles via regional imbalances in the allocation of and demand for capital. Since disequilibrium is the basic cause of cycles, imbalances, in theory at least, can be included among their explanations, though it cannot be expected that their role would be more than marginal.

Finally, there remains a question of replication. In this study only one region has been investigated, with favourable, if not conclusive, results. But East Anglia presents a relatively simple economic landscape and although it might be postulated that regional variables found to be important here will also be significant elsewhere it cannot be predicted with such confidence that their weight in the explanation of cyclical responses will everywhere be the same. Thus, additional regional analysis is necessary before nationally-relevant generalisations can be made.

Conclusion

Finally, this study can be placed in two broad contexts which together form an effective framework for research in regional economic geography.

First, there is increasingly a demand for investigations of the processes of regional change and development, which can only partly be satisfied by studies of spatially aggregated systems with data for isolated times. It ought, also, to be apparent that changes occur in the form of alternating phases of acceleration and deceleration rather than as a simple trend. Adequate descriptions and explanations of processes, therefore, can only be carried out at high levels of disaggregation in time and space. Here, disaggregation has been the keynote, but it would be possible to reconstruct the long-term trends from these medium-term fluctuations and, in doing so, gain deeper insights into the processes by which the former are moulded.

The second context concerns the evolution and verification of theories in economic geography. Rather than develop an entirely novel framework the aim was to bring together, as others have done, theories of economists and economic geographers to produce a new arrangement, out of which the understanding of spatial distributions, found from the data, could be furthered. Such interaction of theories inevitably leaves a certain amount of indeterminacy attributable to the unique element of local economies, but it improves on the explanation of which either, alone, is capable. It has been possible, also, to evaluate some of the hypothetical statements concerning the determinants of regional behaviour. Thus, inter-industrial variations, although important, are not to be seen as the over-riding influence in economic welfare; at least as much importance must be given to intra-industrial components, of which spatial structure and interaction play a most significant role.

No special plea need be made for the study of business cycles in economic geography. They have intrinsic interest for the variations in response evoked among different areas. But, much more than that, as Schumpeter states, economic progress is cyclical, and business cycles provide "the material with which to build the fundamental theory of capitalist reality".[1] If ever a complete understanding of the processes in economic geography is achieved it will be with this statement firmly in mind.

References

1. Schumpeter, J. A. (1954) *History of Economic Analysis*. London. p. 1135.